Japanese Folk-Plays

Scene from " A Bag of Tangerines " (see page 41).

JAPANESE FOLK-PLAYS

The Ink-Smeared Lady and Other Kyogen

translated by
SHIO SAKANISHI

with illustrations by
YOSHIE NOGUCHI

CHARLES E. TUTTLE COMPANY
Rutland, Vermont & Tokyo, Japan

PREFACE

the indispensable objects. Weapons, such as swords, spears, and bows and arrows are represented by actual articles. The illustrations show the costumes generally worn by the actors. The masks made of wood differ according to the different schools, but the *kyôgen* masks are comparatively few in number. Those of Buaku for rogues, of Oto for a female part, of an old man, a young man, a monkey, and a fox are most popularly used.

A list of translations of *kyôgen* in the appendix was originally compiled for the LIST OF TRANSLATIONS OF JAPANESE DRAMA by the author assisted by P. D. Perkins and Marion H. Addington, and was published in mimeographed form by the American Council of Learned Societies in 1935. I have added forty-three titles since then and reprint it with the permission of the Council.

I am greatly indebted to Mr. Sengorô Shigeyama, the present master of the *Ôkura* school of *kyôgen*, and his two sons, for their kindness in posing for the illustration. For the photographs I am obliged to Mr. Tainosuke Nakajima of the Taiseikaku Studio in Kyoto. My gratitude is due to the Kokusai Bunka Shinkokai in granting me a fund to have the plates printed in Japan. To Lilian E. Knowles and Helen Agnes DeLano for many valuable suggestions, and to Laurence Salisbury for assisting me in the final revision of the manuscript, I wish to express my grateful acknowledgment.

Library of Congress
January, 1938

S. S.

NOTE TO THE NEW EDITION

This book was first published some twenty years ago in Boston. It was then, as the reader will see from Dr. Sakanishi's preface to the original edition, the only collection of translations of the Japanese folk-plays known as Kyogen. At that time other isolated translations of Kyogen had already appeared in various books and anthologies. Since then, Kyogen, as well as the more esoteric Noh drama which it usually accompanies, has become more widely known to Westerners. It is still, however, one of the lesser known of Japanese dramatic art forms; and perhaps this is due in part to its colloquialisms and sometimes archaic forms of speech that a Westerner would find difficult to understand. Dr. Sakanishi's excellent translations, however, will help the reader overcome this difficulty to a great extent. Not only are they deft and clear, but they retain the distinctive charm and unpretentious, often earthy humor that characterizes Kyogen. The publishers are happy to be able to bring back into print what is sure to remain for many years one of the ablest and most interesting books on the subject.

1960   The Publishers

CONTENTS

CONTENTS

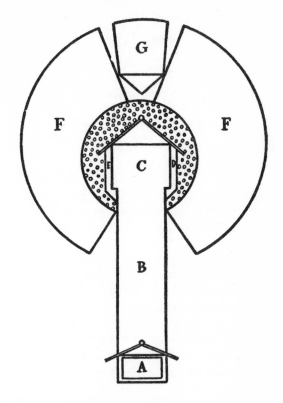

PLAN OF THE SARUGAKU STAGE

- *A* Green room.
- *B* Bridge, a passage for actors.
- *C* Stage.
- *D* Chorus.
- *E* Musicians.
- *F* Audience.
- *G* Shogun and his litter.

KEY TO THE PLAN OF THE MODERN KYÔGEN STAGE

After the Nishi-Honganji Temple in Kyoto
Built by Hideyoshi Toyotomi at the
Close of the Sixteenth Century

A Stage.

B Back-stage.

C Back-wall with a painting of an enormous pine tree.

D Musicians' seats.

E Veranda for chorus.

F Staircase leading to the Shôgun's seat.

G First actor's pillar where he begins his performance.

H Mark-pillar on which the actor fixes his eyes.

I Second actor's pillar to which he withdraws.

J Flute player's pillar.

K Door for chorus, prompters, or actors making a hurried exit.

L Gravel-path to create a sense of detachment between the actors and audience.

M Bridge, a passage for actors.

N Three pine trees to mark position of actors in playing.

O Curtain of five colors.

P Green room.

Q Audience.

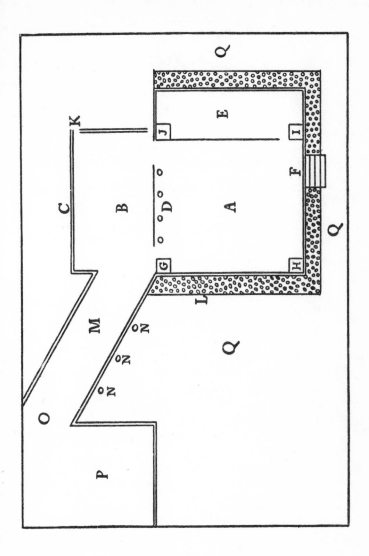

xiii

INTRODUCTION

JAPANESE LITERATURE at an early period, like all literature, was entirely of the folk, and its original setting was a simple, homogeneous society where men of different wealth and rank were extraordinarily similar in their artistic tastes. The earliest Japanese chronicle, *Kojiki*,[1] has preserved for us faithfully the mythology, the manners and customs, the language, and the traditional history of primitive Japan. Her impulse to artistic expression is testified in some two hundred poems scattered through the chronicle, most of which date back to 400 A.D., and although our interest in them is primarily historical rather than literary, they have a certain artless beauty of folk literature.

Half a century later there appeared an anthology of verse, *Manyôshû*.[2] With the exception of a few poems composed in the 4th and 5th centuries, the four thousand poems of the anthology were written during the hundred years before 750, and are the product of a sophisticated culture. Already Indian Buddhism and Chinese culture had permeated the native thought, creating a difference in the tastes of the different classes. Elaborate metaphysics and the artificial psychology of the leisure class were utterly foreign to the experience of the folk, and urban life with its consequent social conventions set up a barrier between the ruler and the ruled, and the city dwellers and the country folk.

The Ashikaga period (1338–1534) with its vitality achieved marvels in bringing two widely separated elements together. After centuries of faithful servitude to the imported culture,

[1] *Kojiki* or "Records of Ancient Matters" was completed in 712 and translated in its entirety by Basil Hall Chamberlain in 1882. The second edition with the late W. G. Aston's annotations was published in 1932.

[2] "Collection of a Myriad Leaves" was probably compiled soon after 750.

1

Japan finally came back to her own, and the age was rife with creative energy which sought its inspiration not in the religious and classical tradition from India or China, but rather in her indigenous culture.   Zen priests and tea masters enjoined upon their followers rustic simplicity and mastery of the truly elemental.   The refined taste came to appreciate the folk ways and folk arts.

Moreover, the time was changing.   The imperial court in Kyoto with its intricate rites and ceremonies was tottering, and the new feudal institutions came to be firmly established.   Some of the chieftains of the new social order, of obscure antecedents in the provinces, had made positions for themselves and were eager to acquire culture and refinement to enhance their dignity and social standing.   On the other hand, various economic changes brought the commoners who had most of the money to a position of real importance.   Each made the best use of what he possessed; hence the military class displayed its power and prestige, while the commoners indulged in their wealth and the pleasures their money could procure.   Their vanity and ambition, nevertheless, contributed much toward the wider diffusion of culture and the breaking down of rigid class distinctions.

Another important factor in the removal of barriers between the classes was the system of patronage by the Shôguns.   Talented artists and skilled artisans often resided on the estates of their patrons and devoted themselves to perfecting their own genius.   Among those who profited most were actors who had led a parasitic existence in temples and shrines.   They were called the *kawara-mono*,[3] "river-bed dwellers," and were considered little better than outcasts.   Now they found themselves in a higher social scale, and the ablest among them began to associate with regents and lords.[4]

[3] The actors were so called, because as strolling players they first gave their performance on the dry river-bed of the Kamo in Kyoto.

[4] For example, Kwanze Kwanami Kiyotsugu (1333–1384) and his son Seami Motokiyo (1364–1444) were taken under the protection of the Shôgun

It was under such circumstances that the *kyôgen* of medieval Japan came to assume the present form. In this short introduction, I shall not be able to give a full history of its origin nor a complete description of modern *kyôgen*. However, through search in old records for references, by deductions and analogies from other types of literature, I hope to reconstruct its background. In a study of this kind, strict proof is not possible nor even desirable, for any one piece of given evidence, often highly debatable, depends much upon one's interpretation. Nevertheless, if the accumulation of small fragments can leave on the reader's mind the total effect of the historical development of the comic interludes, I shall consider my task fulfilled.

ORIGIN

The origin of the *kyôgen* is hidden in obscurity, but there is no doubt that it goes back to some primitive forms of religious worship. Japanese scholars find its beginning in the episode of the sun goddess, Amaterasu, in the *Kojiki*. Offended by the rude pranks of her brother, Prince Susanoo, the great goddess had taken refuge in a rock cave, and the eternal night prevailed on the land. To beguile her from her hiding place, the lesser deities gathered before her cave and made merry with mimic dance and music.[5] Today the myth is more interesting to us as a naïve explanation of a solar eclipse than the origin of dramatic entertainment. It, however, shows that the custom of dance and music before the gods was already ancient at the date of this composition.

Even before historical times, the office of the court jester was assigned to the *Hayabito* from the southwestern corner of Japan. Legend states that when the ancestor of the *Hayabito*, Prince Fire-Shine, once failed to keep his word to his brother, Prince Fire-Subside, the latter took out the tide-flowing jewel to drown

Yoshimitsu Ashikaga (1358–1408) and were treated as if they were the highest officials of the country.

[5] Chamberlain's *Translation of "Kojiki,"* pp. 64–70.

him.   Harassed by the surging waves, Prince Fire-Shine promised that in future his descendants for eighty generations would serve his brother as his mimes. "So down to the present day, his various posturings when drowning are ceaselessly served up," concludes the record.[6] The *Hayabito's* antics provided an element of humor to the otherwise solemn ceremonies of the court and the Shinto shrines.

During the reign of the Empress Suiko, in the year 612, certain Mimashi migrated from Paikché[7] and introduced rhythmic posturing to the beat of drums and other instruments, which then were popular in the Sui court (589–616).   This the Japanese called *sangaku*, taken from the Chinese *san-yäo*, which means "miscellaneous music" or "scattered music" as contrasted to more formal performances.   Music immediately found an ardent exponent in the person of Prince Shôtoku (573–621), the real founder of Buddhism in Japan, and hereafter the court records mention the elaborate programs of music and dancing described as Chinese and Korean at the various religious festivals.   Within the imported arts, however, indigenous folk elements were in time incorporated; consequently, the humorous antics of the *Hayabito*, together with acrobatics, juggling and tumbling, interspersed with impromptu singing and recitation, became so popular that the original name of *sangaku* was corrupted into the more appropriate term of *sarugaku* or "monkey music." Lady Murasaki[8] and Sei Shônagon[9] used the adjective *sarugô gamashi* or "monkeyish" to describe the noisy merry-making of the court.

By the middle of the 11th century, one phase of the *sarugaku* developed into a form of social comedy.   Unfortunately, the

[6] Chamberlain's *Translation of " Kojiki "* pp. 150–151.

[7] One of the three kingdoms of Korea during the middle ages.

[8] *Genji Monogatari* [Tale of Genji] written probably about 1001–1015. Chap. 21.

[9] *Makura no Sôshi* [Pillow-book] written during the years 991–1000. Sections 90, 121, 160.

details of intermediate development are obscure, but during the Kôhei era (1058–1064), a treatise devoted to the dramatic art entitled *Shin Sarugaku ki* or New Notes on *Sarugaku* [10] was written. It is attributed to Akihira Fujiwara (989–1066), scholar and courtier of distinction. According to him, the *sarugaku* is an inclusive term for all types of comic entertainment. Besides those already named, magic, divination, and even fortune-telling are included. In fact, judging from his description, its repertoire was as varied and extensive as that of a large modern circus, and its purpose was "to twist the entrails and dislocate the jaws of its spectators with foolish nonsense." [11]

Akihira's interest, however, is primarily in the farce. Already there had been a definite attempt in characterization and dramatic effect. To quote a few titles from his work: "Priest Fukkô Begs for Robes," "The Nun Myôtaka Asks for Swaddling-clothes," or "A Country Gentleman Goes to the Capital for the First Time." An ignorant but vain priest whose only desire is to own a brocade robe, an indiscreet nun in trouble, and a rustic making himself ridiculous in the city are all stock characters of the later comedies. Moreover, there were actors who specialized in these farcical rôles, and Akihira mentions four or five in the capital. His highest recommendation goes to one Uyemon no Jô in the West Ward of Kyoto, who, assisted by his three wives, sixteen daughters, and eight or nine sons, could present any play with excellent cast. Extemporaneous jokes and gestures were low, if not downright vulgar.

Parallel to the *sarugaku*, there developed the *dengaku*, a rustic sport of the agricultural community. Though very early in its

[10] The text was printed for the first time in the *Gunsho Ruijû*, v. 9, pp. 340–351, from the manuscript dated 1293.

[11] Akihira's contemporary, Takakuni Minamoto (1004–1077), known as the author of the famous *Konjaku Monogatari* [Tales, Ancient and Modern] has the following passage to illustrate this point. As a young courtier tries to make ladies-in-waiting laugh on a bet, one of them says: "Are you going to perform *sarugaku?* That, indeed, would be far better than telling funny stories." v. 24, no. 22, p. 111.

origin, the first description of its performance in literature occurs in the *Eiga Monogatari* [Tales of Glory and Splendour] written by an unknown author of the 11th century. The narrative centers around the brilliant life of Michinaga Fujiwara (966–1027). In the 5th month of the year 1023, Michinaga wished to entertain the mother of Emperor Go Ichijô, who was staying at the Tsuchimikado Palace, and took the imperial party to the scene of rice planting. After the peasant women marched in, there appeared an old man, master of ceremonies, holding a torn umbrella in his hand and clad in a strange garment. He was followed by a group of ten or more *dengaku* performers. With crude drums tied to their waists and drum-sticks in their hands, they marched along in odd gait and played their flutes, while they sang rustic songs and went through various dance motions. The author concludes with the following comment on the event: "Having been used to the most extraordinary and unusual in everything, this rustic scene from real life pleased the noble guest thoroughly." [12]

Dengaku had been under the patronage of the Shinto shrines, and by the mid 12th century, the Kasuga Shrine in Nara and Gion Shrine in Kyoto had professional *dengaku* performers. Later, the military clans under the Kamakura regime (1185–1337), too, maintained their own players. Indeed, that superb master of the *kyôgen*, Tsuchidayû, whose memory Seami speaks of so reverently, was a *dengaku* performer in the service of a feudal lord.[13] After Takatoki Hôjô (1303–1333), the last of the Hôjô Shôguns, however, *dengaku* gradually lost its favor and was superseded by *sarugaku*.

Sarugaku, too, had professional performers attached to such powerful national shrines as the Sumiyoshi in Tamba Province, the Hiyoshi in Ômi, and the Kasuga in Yamato, and by the

---

[12] *Eiga Monogatari*, ed. by K. Sanjônishi. *Iwanami Bunko*, v. 2, sect. 19, pp. 257–258.

[13] *Shûdo-sho* written in 1430. *Seami Jûroku-bu shû*, ed. by Kaizo Nonomura, pp. 232–233. Nothing is known of this *kyôgen* master.

beginning of the 14th century had gone a long way toward becoming a stage play.[14] Much of its "monkeyish" nature had worn off, and the dialogue, aided by music and dancing, could deal successfully with a sustained theme. Nevertheless, the *kyôgen* which had made a gradual growth in the hands of successive authors now had to find a great dramatic genius who was still sufficiently in touch with the folk.

ITS HISTORY AND VICISSITUDES

For the further development of *kyôgen*, the appearance of Kwanami Kiyotsugu and his son, Seami Motokiyo, was extremely timely. As a priest of not very high rank in the Kasuga Shrine, Kwanami's learning could not have been very extensive, but his innate good taste combined with deep respect for the traditional arts made him the most fitting tool to recast his old heritage into a new dramatic form. He gave full credit to former masters such as Icchû, a *dengaku* actor of Ômi,[15] and Inuô, a *sarugaku* master of his contemporary,[16] and profited by their experience. Moreover, his close association with people of high standing and their æsthetic demands helped to lead his sense of dramatic value into the right channel.

It was Kwanami's good fortune to perform in 1374 before the Shôgun Yoshimitsu Ashikaga (1358–1408), who immediately took him under his protection.[17] The young Shôgun was captivated also by his handsome son, Seami, then a boy of

[14] There was a combined performance of the *sarugaku* and *dengaku* on the 11th day of the 6th month in 1349, described in detail in the *Taihei-ki*. *Dai Nihon Shiryô*, Series VI, v. 12, pp. 254–255.

[15] He was the head *kyôgen* master in the performance of 1349, but little is known of his work or life. *Seami Jûroku-bu shû*, pp. 254–255.

[16] A *sarugaku* actor attached to the Hiyoshi Shrine in Ômi Province who died in 1413. His posthumous name is Dôami.

[17] Kwanami then played the rôle of an old man in the *Okina*. *Seami Jûroku-bu shû*, pp. 287–288.

eleven,[18] and granted him honors and privileges of the highest officer. Infuriated by such doings of his lord, Kintada Sanjô (*d.* 1383), then minister of home affairs, wrote in his diary:

> "There has been recently a young *sarugaku* lad from Yamato Province, and our lord is exceedingly fond of him. He shares the same box [19] and eats from the same dish. The *sarugaku* performers are no better than mendicants, but he treats this youth with utmost courtesy and grants many gifts. To win the lord's favor, the feudal dignitaries follow his example and pour countless riches on the lad." [20]

Young as he was, there was enough greatness in Seami not to be spoiled by such excess of favors and protection from the great, but he knew how to profit by his association with the cultivated members of the aristocracy. The Shôgun Yoshimitsu and his coterie were æsthetes who were guided by Zen principles of taste. Both Kwanami and his son, whose intellectual and artistic heritage was meager, willingly accepted the Zen standards of their audience. This is testified to, not in the text of the plays since there is little original writing in them, but in their structure and presentation. Squandering of emotion, exaggerated humor, in fact all that is trite and obvious is avoided; and extreme restraint, rigid convention, and above all the full consciousness of the value of suggestion are substituted. The audience in its turn now is willing to bring knowledge, intellect, and imagination to their creation. It is little wonder that the traditional *sarugaku* and *dengaku* had to be cast into a mould of new æsthetics.

If I have already dwelt on the life and work of these two geniuses inordinately, I have done so purposely. While æsthetic demands of the time were against the "monkeyish" antics of the

---

[18] Seami writes that he was twelve years old then, but that is because of the Japanese way of reckoning. Since he was born in 1363, he was really eleven years old in 1374.

[19] On the 7th day of the 6th month in 1378, Yoshimitsu went to the Gion festival and invited Seami to sit with him.

[20] *Go Gumai-ki*, under the 7th day of the 6th month, 1378.

folk, Kwanami found in the rejected comic element an inspiration, a necessity. While he called the tragic plays of the *sarugaku*, the *Nô*, he named the comic element *kyôgen* or "mad words," and accorded it a permanent place. The *kyôgen*, according to Seami, should "kindle the mind to laughter." [21] It is neither a guffaw nor a horse-laugh of the vulgar, but "a laughter that makes the laugher joyous." [22] To set out to produce laughter is often fatal, for laughter without the comic idea behind it is harsh and soulless. Seami insists on the necessity of restraint and subtle suggestion in *kyôgen*. There should be "a tinge of unreality in reality," and "refinement and concentration of all conflicting qualities into one dominant note." Above all, "neither in speech nor in gesture, should there be anything low. The jokes and repartee should be appropriate even to the ears of the nobles and the refined. However funny they may be, one should never introduce the vulgar. This is of utmost importance to bear in mind." [23]

In his various writings, Seami left no record of the titles or contents of comic interludes. Judging from later records, however, it is safe to assume that the *kyôgen* acquired the present form in Seami's lifetime, for with all the necessary elements at hand, it needed only his definition to limit its scope. The new *sarugaku* was to consist of tragic *Nô* plays followed by comic *kyôgen*. "In olden days," Seami wrote, "four or five plays were given. Even now, it is desirable to give three *Nô* plays and two *kyôgen* in a program. In recent years, however, when we play before the nobles, we are forced to present seven, eight, and even ten plays in one performance, but I do so against my own will." [24]

Twenty years after Seami's death, there was a grand open-air performance of *sarugaku* attended by the high civil and military

---

[21] *Seami Jûroku-bu shû*, pp. 232–234.

[22] It is interesting to compare Seami's notes on *kyôgen* with George Meredith's *An Essay on Comedy*.

[23] *Seami Jûroku-bu shû*, pp. 233–234.

[24] *Ibid.*

dignitaries at Tadasugawara near Kyoto. It began on the 4th day of the fourth month in 1464 and lasted till the 11th. Three days, *i. e.*, the 5th, 7th, and 10th, were devoted to the *Nô* and *kyôgen* and from the two extant manuscripts [25] I will list the titles of *kyôgen* with their translation in square brackets. In case the extant title varies, it will be followed by the present title and its translation. The plays no longer in existence are indicated with an asterisk (*).

FIRST DAY (5th).

Sannomaru Chôja [Three Elders of Sannomaru]

Sannin Chôja [Three Elders]

Saru-hiki [A Monkey-man]

Sarugai Kôtô [An Unfair Exchange]

Kakure Mino [Invisible Cloak]

Oni no Tsuchi [Magic Mallet of the Devil]

Hachi Tataki [Plate Breaking]

Hôraku Wari [Pottery Breaking]

Kwaichû [Pocketing]

Kwaichû Muko [Pocketing son-in-law]

Yawata no mae [In Yawata Village]

SECOND DAY (7th).

Hige Kaitate [Beard-guard]

Hige Yagura

Ka [Mosquito]

Ka-zumô [Mosquito Wrestling]

*Daika Shôka [Big? Little?]

Oni no Mame [Devil's Beans]

Setsubun [The *Setsubun* Festival]

I Moji [Letter "I"]

Jishaku [A Magnet]

[25] *Tadashigawara Kwanjin Sarugaku ki*, dated 1548, and *Ihon Tadashigawara Kwanjin Sarugaku ki*, dated 1583. Printed in the *Gunsho ruijû*, v. 19, pp. 717–721 and 722–723.

THIRD DAY (10th).

Sanbon Bashira [Three Pillars]	*Sannin Bashira* [Pillars for Three]
*Koyomi [Calendar]	
Asahina [Warrior Asahina]	
Cha-gaki Zatô [A Blind Tea-master]	
Hara Tsuzumi [Belly drum]	*Tanuki no Hara Tsuzumi* [Badger's Belly-drum]
Wakame [Seaweed]	
Iruma-gawa [River Iruma]	
Miru Muko [Son-in-law to See]	*Morai Muko* [Son-in-law to Receive]
Karakasa no Shûku [Poems on an Umbrella]	*Shûku Karakasa*
*Wara Uchi [Straw-beating]	
Mochi-kui [Eating Rice-cakes]	*Narihira Mochi* [Narihira's Rice-cakes]

Thus the *kyôgen* at the close of the 15th century became a recognized form of interlude for use in connection with the more stately *Nô*, and under the patronage of the Shogunate it devoted the succeeding two hundred years, first, to acquiring a creditable ancestry by fabricating testimonials and documents, and, second, to establishing its texts.

PROBLEMS OF AUTHORSHIP AND TEXTS

The able *dengaku* and *sarugaku* performers, who had been attached to various shrines in provinces in the 15th century, flocked to the capital, and the regional differences of the folk arts in due time developed into schools, each claiming distinguished ancestry and originality. It is, however, sufficient for our purpose to consider briefly three schools: the *Ôkura*, the *Sagi*, and the *Izumi*, in the order of their appearance.

Toraaki Yaemon Ôkura (*d.* 1662), the thirteenth master of the *Ôkura* school, wrote in 1660 *Waranbe-gusa*, the first treatise wholly devoted to *kyôgen*. In it, he credits Priest Gené (1269–1350) as the first author of these light comedies, and names titles of some fifty-nine plays.[26] To quote: "A certain priest, Enzai Gené, a native of Kyoto and a resident of Mount Hiei, believing that the amusement of mad speeches and jokes, too, could be harnessed into spiritual edification and praise of Buddha, composed many *kyôgen*." [27]

According to Toraaki, Gené was succeeded by the Hiyoshi family in Ômi Province, the guardian of the famous *Ômi sarugaku*. The fifth head of the school, Yatarô Hiyoshi, moved to Nara to join the actors of the Kasuga Shrine, thus bringing together the two famous schools of *sarugaku* in Ômi and Yamato Provinces. This, I believe, took place during the lifetime of Seami.

Toraaki names Shirôjirô Komparu (*ca.* 1500), son of the famous Zenchiku Ujinobu (1414–1499) and grandson of Seami, and his contemporary, Yatarô Uji, as the authors of seventy-eight plays. He further lists twenty-five plays of anonymous authorship. Though to accept his statement is to solve all the perplexing problems of *kyôgen* authorship, there is unfortunately no evidence to substantiate it. Gené, to be sure, was a learned man and a fervent "religioso," and the legend of his authorship of *kyôgen* probably originated from the fact that he sought illustrations for his teaching in the common everyday incidents of life.

The *Ôkura* school really was founded by Shirôjirô Komparu in the early 16th century, and after the decline of the Hôjô regime, it was favored by the famous regent, Hideyoshi Toyotomi (1536–1598). On the 5th day of the 10th month in 1593, Hideyoshi with Ieyasu Tokugawa (1536–1616) and Toshiie Maeda (1538–1596) played the *Mimi-hiki* [Ear-pulling] which is known as the

---

[26] From the stylistic evidence those plays attributed to Gené on the whole are primitive in form and original in content, suggesting earlier composition.

[27] Sasano, Katashi, "*Nô Kyôgen no Shishô.*" *Kokugo To Kokubungaku*, v. 7, no. 4, April, 1930, pp. 457–458.

Kuchi Mane today, and the set of costumes he used was given to Toramasa Yaemon Ôkura (1539–1604), the master of the school at the time. His son, Torakiyo (1566–1646), was granted a small feudal territory.

Ieyasu, who succeeded Hideyoshi in the dictatorship, favored the *Sagi* school founded by Sôgen Ninemon (1508–1598). It is said that Sôgen, by the order of his patron, composed the *Meshisen*, the only *kyôgen* of which the authorship is known, but my search failed to disclose its text in any of the collected works. Throughout the Tokugawa regime (1616–1867) the *Sagi* school enjoyed an exclusive patronage. In spite of the various testimonials and documents that the school managed to produce to enhance its prestige, the *Sagi* is only a branch of the *Ôkura* school and has little originality either in its texts or in performance. It is no wonder that Toraaki Ôkura wrote in his *Waranbe-gusa:* "To call itself a school is ridiculous."

The *Izumi* school was founded by Gensuke Yamawaki (*d.* 1569), who descended from Shirôjirô Komparu, the founder of the *Ôkura* school. In 1614 he was invited to the Owari clan by Lord Yoshinao Tokugawa (1600–1650), who in 1631 made him the governor of Izumi Province from which the school derives its name. Mototada Yamawaki (1747–1816), the sixth master, went to Edo where he came into close contact with the masters of other schools, and revised all the texts of his school. His manuscript came to be known as *Kumogata-bon* [Cloud-pattern Book] from its cover design. It lists two hundred plays.

A member of the *Izumi* school established a branch known as the *Nomura* school. Little is known of its founder or the school, but in its possession, there is another important *kyôgen* manuscript known as the *Namigata-bon* [Wave-pattern Book] so named from its cover design. The *Namigata-bon* with two hundred and fifty-two plays probably antedates the *Kumogata-bon* and furnishes many interesting textual comparisons.

The problems of *kyôgen* texts are as perplexing as those of its authorship. The *kyôgen* is to be seen on the stage and not to be read. Originally its various themes as well as dialogues were handed down orally from one master to the other, and there was no text; its actor was also its author. Seami wrote: "As to an officer of the *kyôgen*, his chief function is that of a merrymaker, a drawing-room jester, who makes up an entertaining scene by means of old anecdotes and incidents." [28] This is an excellent definition of the *kyôgen* of the time, and long after it came under the patronage of the military clique, it retained to a great extent its original quality. In the beginning of the 18th century Hakuseki Arai (1657–1725) wrote:

> "In the time of Lord Muromachi [29] by a performance of the *kyôgen* it meant, not presenting a play which already existed, but rather an impromptu performance of something amusing for that particular occasion. A nobleman who hates to have his hair dressed is Lord Kamakura,[30] and those who lap up flattery of very obvious kinds are the nobles of Kyoto." [31]

Sometimes the *kyôgen* had a more practical purpose to fulfill. Hamlet's use of the stage was tried also by the Japanese. When a counsel to a wayward lord was too dangerous, his attendants served up his vice on the *kyôgen* stage so that he could see himself objectively. The Buddhist temples, too, employed it to make religious experience easier for the common people to accept.[32]

The facts mentioned above go to prove the extremely flexible quality of the *kyôgen*. Seami undoubtedly contributed much toward its final form. Already in the *sarugaku* performance of 1464, out of twenty-three plays given, twenty have come down

[28] *Seami Jûroku-bu shû*, pp. 232–233.

[29] Yoshimitsu Ashikaga (1358–1408), Shôgun and patron of Kwanami and Seami.

[30] Yoritomo Minamoto (1147–1199), founder of the Kamakura Shogunate.

[31] *Haiyû-kô* [On Actors] *Kobunko*, v. 6, p. 414.

[32] Engaku Shônin in the 14th century introduced the *kyôgen* at Mibu, and some thirty plays were handed down in oral tradition in the temple. Even today there is an annual performance of the *Mibu kyôgen*. Some of them are didactic while the others have no relation to Buddhist teaching.

to us. On the other hand, there is every reason to believe that they were handed down only in general outline and dialogue. Hence any able master could mould them with great freedom and originality to suit the occasion, and the revised versions were handed down in their improved forms. Under such circumstances the *kyôgen* actors were not greatly concerned with actually writing them down, and if they were recorded by some chance, they were in the form of memoranda and never a complete text of any one play.

It was Toraaki Ôkura who first took pains to write the texts of two hundred and three *kyôgen* in 1638. He classified them in eight major groups according to subjects, and in the preface he states:

> "Under no circumstances should this manuscript be shown to strangers. Since I am not naturally bright, I fear I may forget what my father has taught me. Hence I write these plays down. There may be some who blame my doing so, but I shall appreciate those who think my task creditable." [33]

Toraaki is most apologetic of his task. In the postscript, he further writes:

> ". . . Previous to this, the plays were handed down from generation to generation by oral tradition and never have been recorded. I fear, however, in due time they may become so far removed from the original that they cannot be recognized. . . ." [34]

This is dated "the 9th month, 1642," probably the date Toraaki completed his stupendous task, and is followed by an endorsement by his father, Torakiyo Yaemon Ôkura (1566–1646), testifying to the absolute accuracy of the texts of the oral tradition. It is dated "the first month of the year 1645," a few months before his death. This episode of the first recording of the *kyôgen* is narrated with ritual solemnity.

[33] Sasano, Katashi. "*Nô Kyôgen no Shishô.*" *Kokugo To Kokubungaku,* v. 7, no. 4, pp. 457–488.   [34] *Ibid.*

Toraaki believed, and rightly too, that the themes and dialogues of the *kyôgen* in the hands of successive masters had reached the point where further improvement was neither possible nor desirable, and wished to give it permanent form. It was, however, destined to go through further changes. In 1792, Torahiro Yaemon Ôkura (1758–1805), the nineteenth master of the school, transcribed the texts anew. A close comparison of the two discloses an amazing number of differences, and although they are minor, nevertheless, from the point of textual collation, they are of enough significance to be noted.

An ambitious publisher in Edo in 1660 printed the first texts of one hundred and fifty *kyôgen* in five small volumes. It was well illustrated with sketches of scenes from various plays. The work was popular and went through the second edition in two years. It is entitled the *kyôgen-ki* [*Kyôgen* Records]. The question is, where did the publisher obtain the texts? All the schools jealously hid theirs, and if an occasion necessitated that one school borrow a text of another school, the two masters exchanged an oath, first, to be faithful to the text, and, second, not let it fall into the hands of any other school. The *Kyôgen-ki*, in fact, cannot be said to belong to any one school. It seems that it is made up of shorthand notes taken at the *kyôgen* performances. There is much that is attributed to the *Ôkura* school followed by the *Izumi* school element; the *Sagi* and other minor schools are almost negligible. The earlier scholars took these printed editons as their authority for the textual study of the *kyôgen*. This is no longer so. For their comparative study, they must go to the manuscripts which, unfortunately, are in the possession of private families and not yet available.

SOURCES

I have already stated how homogeneous the primitive society of the island empire was, and even long after the importation of new culture, the folk adhered to their simple life and living. With a keen eye for character and an equally keen appreciation of any deviations from the normal in their midst, they could laugh at subtle things. The virago, the drunkard, the cowardly *samurai*, the ignorant feudal lord, the sly servant, and the shrew — all afforded them a great deal of pleasure; and at the annual festival of the local shrine, in a holiday mood, the talented among them took off the absurdity of their fellow men. The themes of the *kyôgen*, indeed, are the obvious everyday experiences of simple personalities.

There are, however, some *kyôgen* which have definite literary sources. The *Busu*, for example, comes from a Buddhist example-book, *Shaseki-shû* [Sand and Pebbles],[35] compiled by Priest Muju (*d.* 1312). A monk too greedy to share a jar of malt syrup with his acolyte loses out at the end just as the feudal lord in the *Busu* loses not only his precious "Busu" but also his priceless art treasures.

The plot of the *Ink-smeared Lady* is from an incident mentioned in Lady Murasaki's *Tale of Genji*. When Murasaki was trying to wipe off a dab of red which Genji put on his nose, "Take care," he cried laughing, "that you do not serve me as Heichu was treated by his lady. I would rather have a red than a black nose."[36] Heichu, referred to here, used to splash his cheeks with water from a little bottle in order that his lady might think he was weeping at her unkindness. She exposed this device by mixing ink with the water.

As interludes, the *kyôgen* sometimes parodied the serious *Nô* drama. The *Bird-catcher in Hades* is a parody of the *Ukai* [The Cormorant-fisher] by Enami no Sayemon (*ca.* 1400). It is against the Buddhist law to take life; therefore the cormorant-fisher in the *Nô* play and the bird-catcher in the *kyôgen* are destined to the torture of hell-fire, but because the former once gave lodging to a wandering priest and the latter fed the demons with his catch, the cormorant-fisher is carried to the presence of Buddha while the bird-catcher gets a new lease on life.

[35] Book VII, part 2, no. 16.
[36] Chapter VI, *Suyetsumu-hana* [The Saffron Flower], the last paragraph.

The *kyôgen*, as folk-play, often found its inspiration in folk-lore. The bewitching fox, the pot-bellied badger, the thunder god with a string of drums, and the devils from the Island of Eternal Youth are the familiar characters. Especially the horned and saw-toothed devil is human and even lovable. On his way to the Dragon's Day fair, he accosts Jimbei and Gohei as his travelling companions. Unfortunately they are frightened.

"Oh, terrible, terrible! Please spare our lives."

The amiable devil replies:

"Come, come, my dear fellows! I am not so terrible. I am a devil from the Island of Eternal Youth."

Such a confirmation is not at all comforting to them, and Jimbei cries:

"But if the devil is not frightening, what is?"

With the assurance that he is "not the kind that eats such a foul thing as man," their minds are put at ease, and their friendship is established.

It is interesting to note that many extant paintings from Ôtsu of the 17th and 18th centuries deal with the same subjects treated in the *kyôgen*. Produced by the folk in the folk tradition, these paintings, like the dialogue of the *kyôgen*, attained genuine simplicity and spontaneity as well as a marked degree of technical skill. Only common people in the grip of common tradition could produce such an unsigned and undated literary or artistic work. I shall attempt neither their analysis nor comparison, but merely enumerate the subjects which are common to both. A monkey man with his beast, a devil chased by a mouse with a holly twig in its mouth, a thunder god who lost his drum in the ocean, a blind man with a musical instrument strapped to his back, Fukurokuju and Daikoku wrestling (a contest between happiness and longevity), a courtesan outwitting a picaro, a beggar, a hawker, and a cut-purse, all these are made articulate, one through the medium of lines and color, and the other by means of vocabulary fresh with imagery.

ÆSTHETIC VALUE OF THE KYÔGEN

What, we may now ask, is the æsthetic value of these comic interludes? The Japanese have been praised or condemned, alternately, for their having or not having good sense of humor till they have come to the conclusion that "serious ideas do for export," but "a nation's fun is for home consumption only." [37] Transported across the border, their humor evaporates into thin air. They, however, admit that humor is the same the world over; only the difference of manners and customs creating the difference in expression.

The characters in the *kyôgen* are few: the principal actor *shite* and his adjuncts *waki* which seldom are more than three. The first actor who comes on the stage announces himself:

"I am a notorious highwayman who resides in this neighborhood."

Or:

"As you are aware, I have been a bachelor for these many years."

The serious audience who has sat through the haunting tragedy of the *Nô* drama is immediately put in the right comic frame of mind without any further forcible coloring. Laughter arises not from any quality or relation of characters but rather in the state of their mind implicit in the observance of rigid stage conventions.

Take, for example, the mirth-provoking Taro Boy. He is spirited enough, but moves within an extraordinarily narrow groove, and the readers of the *kyôgen* who have not seen it acted on the stage may think him very stereotyped, but to the Japanese he is a familiar character. When his master tells him to call when the fowl cries, he asks if a hen will do, and too sleepy to keep his eyes open, he calls his master to tell him that a cock yawned. Taro is always clever and outwits his master in every

[37] Chamberlain, Basil Hall. *Things Japanese*, p. 193.

turn.   Though conventionalized, the mere sight of him vivifies the comic spell.

The comic nature of the plot in the *kyôgen* is most frequently physical; it is a matter of situation rather than character.   Hence incongruity and mistakes produce an emotional shock, and the audience laughs.   In the *Ribs and the Cover*, the priest's instruction to his stupid novice comes just one step behind the actual situation. Therefore, when the man comes to borrow a horse, the novice delivers the speech which he was supposed to use when someone comes to borrow an umbrella.   He delivers the speech on a horse to a man who later comes to invite the priest to a dinner. This is an age-old method used to produce laughter.[38]

The Japanese from early times made good use of repetition and exaggeration.   In the year 484 when Chief Wodate became governor of Harima Province, there was a great feast.   In the course of the evening when two children were made to dance, one of them said:

"Do thou the elder brother dance first."

The elder brother said:

"Do thou the younger brother dance first."

They kept this up several times and the company laughed heartily.[39]   This type of excessive courtesy often was used in the *kyôgen*.   When the country gentleman in the *Gargoyle* stops lamenting over his homely wife, he decides to laugh, and turning to his attendant, says:

"Come, you laugh first."

Innate politeness forbids Taro from doing such a thing.

"No, sir!   Please, you first."

They repeat this several times before they finally burst out laughing, but long before they do, the audience is in hearty laughter.

[38] The same method is used in "Der gescheidte Hans" in the *Kinder und Hausmarchen* by the Brothers Grimm.

[39] Chamberlain's *Translation of* "*Kojiki*," p. 397.

Popular superstitions played an important part in the *kyôgen*. I have already mentioned the rôle of devils or Japanese *oni* in the folk-lore. The *Tangerine Dealer* and the *Aunt's Sake* are based on the fright of the *oni*. The descent of the Niwô in the *Deva King* is based on popular belief in the efficacy of this deity.

Unlike the Western comedy, there is little trace of love interest in the *kyôgen*, for a Japanese takes the relation of man and woman as a matter of fact and attaches to it no romance. His marriage is arranged, and his wife is a necessary unit in that social institution called family. This sentiment is well expressed in the words of the country gentleman of the *Gargoyle*:

> "I was a fool to get so wrought up over my homely wife
> in the country. Though I cannot care for her, she has
> given me many marvelous sons who are my wealth and
> future hope. That is wondrously lucky for me."

It has often been asked how the feudal regime tolerated the *kyôgen* to be played at their official functions, for more than half of the extant plays deal with the members of the feudal clan in a not too favorable light. The braggart, the coward, the fop, and the hypocrite all appear as feudal lords. Some scholars claim that the so-called feudal lords in the *kyôgen* are the poverty-stricken and degenerated courtiers of Kyoto in disguise; hence the feudal dignitaries took a great delight in the plays. The explanation, however, is slightly strained when one considers how a *kyôgen* master in 1424 was severely punished because he staged a play depicting the destitute condition of the nobles in the imperial court.[40]

Feudal lords of the *kyôgen* to me are feudal lords, and none other. Here we touch upon the perplexing problem of aesthetics. Professor Parker says:

> "The comical object, the thing that makes us laugh or
> smile and gives us the pleasure of laughter and smiling,
> is the thing which emphatically contrasts with what is

[40] *Kambun Nikki* [Things Seen and Heard] under the 11th day, 3rd month, 1424.

> usual, expected, conventional, right, and true — with
> all those values therefore which make up the civilized
> part of man's nature. The comical thing is the unusual,
> unexpected, unconventional, wrong, and false — in
> the large sense of the word, it is evil." [41]

How comic is the blind man whose wife left him, leaving behind a
monkey in *An Unfair Exchange!* How ridiculous is the husband
who is dragged across the stage by his wife with a bag over his
head in the *Bag of Parting!* They are pathetic, but we laugh at
them. In fact often we cannot help laughing at them. The
only satisfactory explanation advanced so far is the theory of
"psychical distance" between us and the evil things. Evil must
not touch us personally, or else we lament instead of laughing.
The nobles of Kyoto who were making desperate effort to conceal
their mental and physical bareness could not see themselves
impersonally. Even gentle ridicule cut them to the core. On
the other hand, the feudal dignitaries in power were so full of
the sense of their superiority and risibility over any unfortunate
butt that they could side against themselves and laugh at their
own absurdity.

Much can be written about the *kyôgen*, but these translated
plays themselves speak more eloquently than anything that can
be said. The real contribution of the *kyôgen* to Japanese literature
lies in its homely humor, which is not the French *esprit*, born of
high intellect and pure sophistication ; nor is it the Anglo-Saxon
notion of comic as the fountain-head of sound sense. For, to the
Japanese, the former is tortured with self-consciousness, while
the latter with its irony and self-criticism has a sobering effect.
Japanese humor under all circumstances is thoroughly artless
and permanently human.

[41] Parker, DeWitt Henry. *The Analysis of Art*, p. 120.

KYÔGEN

COMIC INTERLUDES OF JAPAN

THE INK–SMEARED LADY
(Suminuri Onna)

Characters: A FEUDAL LORD, TARO, *his attendant*, THE LORD'S MISTRESS.

LORD.   I am a famous feudal lord of a distant province. I have been in the capital very long on a lawsuit, but finally it was decided in my favor, and luckily a vast new territory was added to my possession. Nothing delights me more than this. First I will call Taro boy and share the joy of this auspicious event with him.

Yai, yai! Is Taro boy around?

TARO.   *Ha!*

LORD.   Where are you?

TARO.   In your presence.

LORD.   It is nothing special. Our long stay in the capital comes to an end with the court decision in my favor. A vast new territory was added to my possession. Is not this a very happy day?

TARO.   It is indeed a happy day. I wish to congratulate you.

LORD.   Now this means that I have to go home soon. That, by the by, reminds me I must make a farewell call on my lady in town, for once back in the province, I do not know when I can see her again. What do you think?

23

TARO.   That will be a very good plan, sir.

LORD.   Then I shall go.   You accompany me.

TARO.   Very well.

LORD.   Come!

TARO.   I am coming!

LORD.   When my wife in the province hears this good news, she will be waiting for my home-coming day and night.

TARO.   She must, indeed.
    Oh, sir, we are already here.   Shall I announce your arrival? Please wait here.

LORD.   All right.

TARO.   Please, your lord has come.

MISTRESS.   *Ha!*   There is an unfamiliar voice outside.
    Oh, is that you, Taro?   My lord is here, did you say?

TARO.   Yes, madam.

MISTRESS.   Oh!   This is most unexpected.   Pray, what lucky wind has brought you here?   How have you been?   As I had not seen you for a long while, I had certain misgivings.

LORD.   Oh, I am happy to find you well.   I have not seen you for a long while, have I?
    By the by, Taro boy, shall I tell her about our news?

TARO.   I believe there is no harm in telling her that.

MISTRESS.   What could it be?   Oh, I have fears.

LORD.   Oh, no!   It is nothing very important.   We have been in the capital for a long while about the lawsuit, but finally it was decided in our favor today.   As I must be going home soon, I came to say farewell.

MISTRESS.   Alas, what do I hear?   Going back home!   Then I shall not be able to see you again.   How sad this is!   (*She secretly draws to her a little water basin in the writing box.   Putting a few drops on her face, she pretends to cry bitterly.*)

LORD. Your deep grief touches me, but even if I go home, I shall be coming back soon. Therefore be of good cheer and wait for me. (*He weeps too.*)

MISTRESS. You say so now, but once back home, you will not even think of me. This is very sad indeed.

TARO. What do I see? I thought she was really crying, but she is just putting water on her face. What an odious shrew she is!

Pardon me, my lord! Will you come this way just a moment?

LORD. What is the matter?

TARO. Do you think she is really weeping? If you do, you are wrong. That's only plain water from the writing box.

LORD. Don't talk such nonsense to me! The poor thing is really crying because she must part with me.

MISTRESS. Oh, my dear lord! Where have you gone? 'Tis only a little while we can be together. Please come here.

LORD. I am sorry. Taro boy had something to tell me, so I went over there. The fool was talking nonsense.

TARO. It's incredible not to see through the woman's trick. Well, I have a scheme. We will see who is right. (*Removing the water basin, he puts an ink-well in its place.*)

MISTRESS. I am so loath to part with you even a few hours, but now this is going to be our last meeting! Oh, so very sad and miserable!

TARO. This is fun. Not knowing my trick, now she is putting ink all over her face. Just look at that face!

Oh, please, my lord! Will you step this way just a moment?

LORD. What is the matter?

TARO. Because you did not believe what I told you, I replaced the water basin with an ink-well. Just look at that face, please!

LORD. You are right, my boy! I was a fool to be so easily tricked and duped. What can I do to that deceitful woman? Oh, yes. I will give her my hand-mirror as a keepsake. That ought to put her to shame.

TARO. That is a splendid idea.

LORD. Well, when I go home and settle down, I shall send for you as soon as possible, but till then I shall leave this mirror as a keepsake. Treasure it. Here, please accept my gift.

MISTRESS. Oh, I am so wretched! I never thought I should have to accept a keepsake from you. This is a melancholy life indeed. (*She looks in the mirror.*)
What! Who smeared ink on my face? How maddening! Did you do it?

LORD. Oh, no! I know nothing about it. That's Taro's devilment.

MISTRESS. That's not going to excuse you. You cannot get away so easily as that. I must smear your face. (*She smears him.*)

LORD. It is outrageous to blacken my face. Forgive me, forgive me. (*He runs away.*)

MISTRESS. Hey, Taro, where are you? I will blacken your dirty face, too. (*She catches Taro.*)

TARO. It is terrible to have my face blackened like this. Pardon, pardon!

MISTRESS. Never, never! Don't let the rascal get away. Catch him, catch him!

THE RIBS AND THE COVER
(*Hone-kawa*)

Characters: THE PRIEST, THE NOVICE, THE FIRST VISITOR, THE SECOND VISITOR, THE THIRD VISITOR.

PRIEST.   I am the priest of this temple. I have something to say to my assistant.   Is the novice around?   Where are you?

NOVICE.   Right here.   What do you wish?

PRIEST.   It is nothing special. But as I grow older I feel weary of bearing many burdens. This very day I am going to retire and make you responsible for the temple.

NOVICE.   I am indeed greatly obliged to you for this honor, but I have not gone very far in my learning.   Perhaps it would be better not to decide upon this important matter just now.

PRIEST.   I call that a very gracious answer. But even if I retire, I shall be right here, and if any important matter comes up, you can always consult me.

NOVICE.   In that case, I will obey your command.

PRIEST.   Needless to say, you must try to find favor in the eyes of our patrons and make the temple prosperous.

NOVICE.   Rest assured.   I shall do my best.

PRIEST.   That's good.   I am retiring now.   If you wish to ask me anything, come and do so.   If any patrons call, let me know.

NOVICE.   Very good, sir.

Well, well!   I have been wondering when the priest intended to retire, but never suspected that such good luck would befall me this very day.   The patrons of the temple will be happy to hear this, and I shall do my best to win their good will.

FIRST VISITOR. I am a villager who dwells in this vicinity. I am on my way to do an errand. But the sky turns dark suddenly, and I fear it is going to rain. I will stop at my temple and borrow an umbrella. Oh, here I am. Please! Please!

NOVICE. How do you do? I am very happy to see you.

FIRST VISITOR. I have been neglecting to call, but how is the priest? And you? I hope you are both well.

NOVICE. We are both very well. By the by, the priest has decided to retire, giving me full responsibility for the temple. Please come often.

FIRST VISITOR. I congratulate you! Had I known, I should have come especially to wish you success.

As to my present visit, I was on my way to the village, but suddenly it looked as if it were going to rain. Could you let me have an umbrella?

NOVICE. Certainly. Please wait a moment.

FIRST VISITOR. Oh! Very many thanks.

NOVICE. Here, then! I will let you have this.

FIRST VISITOR. Thank you so much.

NOVICE. If there is anything of any kind that I can do for you, please let me know.

FIRST VISITOR. Certainly. I will call on you for assistance.

NOVICE. Are you going?

FIRST VISITOR. Yes. Good-bye!

NOVICE. Good-bye!

FIRST VISITOR. I am much obliged to you.

NOVICE. I am glad you came in.

FIRST VISITOR. Ah! Well! I am glad I did.
Now I must hurry.

NOVICE. The priest told me to let him know if any of the patrons came. I will go and tell him.
Please, sir! Are you in?

PRIEST. Yes, I am here.

NOVICE. You must be feeling very dull.

PRIEST. No, not very.

NOVICE. Somebody has just been here.

PRIEST. Did he come to worship, or was it that he had some business?

NOVICE. He came to borrow an umbrella, and I let him have one.

PRIEST. That was quite right, but tell me. Which umbrella did you let him have?

NOVICE. The new one that we got the other day.

PRIEST. You are a careless fellow. Would anybody ever dream of lending an umbrella which I have not used yet? The case will present itself again. When you do not wish to lend it, you can always find a good excuse.

NOVICE. What would you say?

PRIEST. You should say: "It would be no trouble to lend it to you, but recently my master went out with it and encountered a gust of wind at the crossing. The storm tore the ribs and the cover apart. So I tied them both by the middle and hung them up to the ceiling. I am afraid they would be of little use to you." You should say something like that, with an air of truth about it.

NOVICE. I understand. Next time I shall certainly remember what you have told me.
Now I must go.

PRIEST. Must you go? Good-bye!

NOVICE. Good-bye!
That is very queer. Whatever my master says, it does seem strange to refuse to lend a thing when you have it by you.

SECOND VISITOR. I live in this vicinity. As I have to go to a far-off place, I mean to stop at the temple and borrow a horse. I will go quickly. Ah! Here I am. Please! Please!

NOVICE. There is someone calling at the gate again. Who is asking for admittance? Who is calling?

SECOND VISITOR. It is I.

NOVICE. How do you do? I am happy to see you.

SECOND VISITOR. My present reason for calling you is just this. I am going to a far-off place today, and though it is a bold request to make, I should be greatly obliged if you could let me have your horse.

NOVICE. Nothing could be slighter than your request. But unfortunately a few days ago my master went out with it and encountered a gust of wind at the crossing. The storm tore the ribs and the cover apart. So I tied them by the middle and hung them up to the ceiling. I am afraid they would be of little use to you.

SECOND VISITOR. But I am speaking of the horse.

NOVICE. Precisely. I, too, am speaking about the horse.

SECOND VISITOR. Well! Then there is no help for it. I must be going.

NOVICE. Must you go?

SECOND VISITOR. Yes! Good-bye!

NOVICE. I am so glad you dropped in. Good-bye!

SECOND VISITOR. Well! I never! He says things that I cannot at all understand.

NOVICE. As I told this man exactly what the priest told me to say, I am sure my master will be pleased.
   Pardon me! Are you in?

PRIEST. Yes, I am in. What can I do for you?

NOVICE. Someone has just been here to borrow a horse.

PRIEST. Fortunately no one is using it today. Did you let him take it?

NOVICE. Oh, no! I told him exactly what you had instructed me to say.

PRIEST.   What! I do not remember saying anything about the horse. What did you tell him?

NOVICE.   I said that a few days ago my master went out with it and encountered a gust of wind at the crossing; that the storm tore the ribs and the cover apart. So I tied them by the middle and hung them up to the ceiling. I was afraid they would be of little use to him.

PRIEST.   What do you mean? That was what I told you to say when someone came to borrow an umbrella. But would anybody ever dream of saying such a thing to a person who would come to borrow a horse? When you do not wish to lend it, you can make a fitting excuse.

NOVICE.   Tell me what I should say.

PRIEST.   You should say: "We have recently put our horse out to spring grass, and he has gone stark mad, breaking his hip bone. Just at present he is lying in the corner of the stable under a straw mat. I fear he is not going to be of much service to you." You should say something like that, with an air of truth about it.

NOVICE.   I shall keep it in mind. Next time I shall say something like that.

PRIEST.   Be sure you do not say anything stupid.

NOVICE.   What can this mean? I was ordered to say it, and when I did say it, I got a scolding! This is the most troublesome thing.

THIRD VISITOR.   I am a resident in this neighborhood, and I am on my way to the temple where I have some business. Ah! Here I am. Please! Please!

NOVICE.   There is someone calling at the gate again. Who is that asking for admittance? Who is it?

THIRD VISITOR.   It is I.

NOVICE.   Oh, I am so glad you came.

THIRD VISITOR.   I have not called on you for a long time.   I hope both the priest and you have been well.

NOVICE.   Oh, yes! We both continue well. By the by, I do not know what prompted the priest, but suddenly he has turned the whole responsibility of the temple to me and retired. I hope you will come as often as before.

THIRD VISITOR.   I congratulate you indeed. Had I known it, I should have come especially to congratulate you.

Today I came on business. Tomorrow is the religious anniversary of our family, and I shall be greatly honored if both the priest and you can come.

NOVICE.   To be sure, I can. As to the priest, I am afraid he cannot come.

THIRD VISITOR.   Has he a previous engagement?

NOVICE.   No! But recently we have been putting him out to spring grass, and he has gone stark mad and has broken his hip bone. At present he is lying in the corner of the stable under a straw mat. I fear he is not going to be of very much service to you.

THIRD VISITOR.   But it is the priest that I am talking about.

NOVICE.   Precisely! I am speaking about the priest.

THIRD VISITOR.   Well! I am very sorry to hear that. Then you will come?

NOVICE.   Most certainly, I will come.

THIRD VISITOR.   Now I must go.

NOVICE.   Must you? Good-bye!

THIRD VISITOR.   Well, well! He says things that I cannot make out at all.

NOVICE.   This time I did as I was instructed, and the priest ought to be pleased.

If you please, are you in?

PRIEST.   Yes, I am in. Is it on business that you come?

NOVICE. Somebody has just been here to ask both you and me to go to him tomorrow to attend a religious anniversary in his family. So I said that I would go, but that you would hardly be able to do so.

PRIEST. Luckily I have no engagement tomorrow, and I should like to go.

NOVICE. But I said what you had instructed me to say.

PRIEST. I do not remember. What did you tell him?

NOVICE. I said that you had been put out to spring grass, but had gone stark mad and broken your hip bone. At present you were lying in the corner of the stable under a straw mat. I said I feared that you could not come.

PRIEST. Did you really and truly say that to him?

NOVICE. Yes! Really and truly.

PRIEST. Well, I never! Say what you will, you are a perfect dunce. No matter how many times I say a thing, nothing seems to make you understand. I told you to say that when anyone came to borrow a horse.

The end of all this is that it will never do for you to become a priest. Get out!

NOVICE. Oh!

PRIEST. Won't you get out? Won't you get out? Won't you?

NOVICE. Ouch! ouch! o-u-c-h!

But, sir! Even if you are my master, it is a great shame for you to beat me like this. For all you are the man you are, you cannot tell me that you have not gone stark mad.

PRIEST. When have I ever gone stark mad? If I ever was, out with it quick! Out with it!

NOVICE. If I were to tell it, you would be put to shame.

PRIEST. I know of nothing that could put me to shame. If there is, out with it quick, quick!

NOVICE. Well then, I will tell it.

PRIEST. Hurry up!

NOVICE. Well! A while ago Mistress Ichi who lives across from the temple gate came to call . . .

PRIEST. What has Ichi got to do with me?

NOVICE. But please listen! You beckoned to her and disappeared with her into your dwelling quarters. Do you not call a priest who did such a thing stark mad?

PRIEST. You rascal! Inventing things I never did, you put your master out of countenance. After this, by the Hachiman God with his bow and arrows, I shall not let you escape me.

NOVICE. Even if you are my master, I cannot be put down so easily as that.

BOTH. Ah! ah! ah!

NOVICE. Have you learned a lesson? Oh! I am happy. I've won. I've won.

PRIEST. Hey, hey! Where are you going after putting your master in such a plight?

Is there no one there? Catch him! Do not let him get away!

BUAKU

Characters: A FEUDAL LORD, TARO, *his house-boy*, BUAKU, *his servant in disgrace.*

LORD. I am a renowned feudal lord of this country. As I have an unfaithful servant, I will command Taro, my house-boy, to go and bind him up.

Is Taro around?

TARO. *Ha!* In your presence.

LORD. Quick, for once! It's nothing special that I want you for. Go at once and bring Buaku with his hands and feet bound.

TARO. Oh, my lord! Since he is an exceedingly clever fellow, I fear I shall not be able to get him so easily as that.

LORD. Well then, bring his head back.

TARO. I tremble and obey. But my sword is dull and useless. Please lend me yours.

LORD. Very well. Here it is! Make haste and do not fail to carry out my command.

TARO. Very well, sir. (*Exit* LORD.)

This is indeed a troublesome command. But there is no way out. I must go.

Oh, I am already here! Pardon, is anyone inside?

BUAKU. How strange! That sounds very familiar. Who is it? Oh, is it you, Taro boy?

TARO. It is I. Are you in?

BUAKU. *Yai*, Taro boy! Since I have incurred my lord's displeasure, I presume you have come at his command to play a trick on me. I shall not trust you.

35

TARO.   Why, what a funny notion! To tell you the truth we
are all on your side. We have all been saying that our lord
is very unfair to treat poor Buaku so severely, who has long
been in his service, and we have been trying to put in a good
word for you. Now this afternoon the lord is planning to have
a fishing party on the river's bank. Why can't you come and
present your catch to him? We will do our part to set you
right with our lord, too. Come quickly.

BUAKU.   That certainly is very good of you, and I am happy
to have this chance. I will come. Will you go with me?

TARO.   All right. We shall hasten.

BUAKU.   Here we are already. This is an excellent place.
Oh, what an abundance of fish! But I am very unfortunate.
I was so excited that I forgot to bring a net with me.

TARO.   That is surely very unfortunate. What had we better
do?

BUAKU.   Oh, I know how to snare them in the tall grass.
Come, you drive them from that direction, and I will chase
them from the deep water into the grass.

TARO.   Very well.

BUAKU.   I am coming from this direction and you . . .

TARO.   Pardon! 'Tis the lord's command. Prepare yourself.

BUAKU.   Alas, Taro my boy! I thought you were true to me
when I followed you. This is like sewing up a bird's eye only
to let it fly away. If you had only told me at home! There
were a few things I should have liked to tell my wife and
children. Now I cannot even bid them farewell. Poor
things! Well, never mind. What must be, must be. Come
quickly, and kill me.

TARO.   Your grief touches me. Changeable indeed are the
affairs of men. Today this is your fate, but who knows,
tomorrow it may be mine. Wretched is the lot of a court
servant!

BUAKU.   Let me reflect no longer on the trickery of fortune. Come and take at once this worthless head of mine.

TARO.   No, I have changed my mind. I cannot kill you. (*Both begin to weep.*) Pray, flee from the capital at once.

BUAKU.   Do not prolong this agony. Put me out of my misery immediately.

TARO.   While there is life, there is hope. Escape at once.

BUAKU.   Then are you in earnest?

TARO.   Indeed I am.

BUAKU.   Then I will. Pray see that all goes well with my family after I am gone.

TARO.   That I will. But do not lose even a second. Farewell.

BUAKU.   Farewell. (*Exit* TARO.)
     I have barely escaped the mouth of a crocodile. Farewell to the imperial capital! Before I take leave of this beloved city, however, I will bend my way to the temple of Kiyomizu and pay my last homage.

TARO.   I must hasten to my lord.
     Here I am. Is my lord in?

LORD.   *Yai, yai!* What about it? Did you carry out my command?

TARO.   Indeed I did.

LORD.   How did you do it?

TARO.   That is a long story. Buaku is a good hand at every art of self-defense while I am absolutely no good at all. Therefore I had to resort to trickery. First I told him that his fellow servants were eager to have him restored to your favor again, and that you were planning a river party this afternoon, which he ought to consider a heaven-sent opportunity. Why could he not come there so that we could plead for him? Upon hearing this, simple Buaku was so delighted that he virtually ran all the way to the river, and to present to you a good catch, he rushed into deep water. As he was wading through, I pounced upon him, and alas, that was the end of Buaku.

But what an uncommonly sharp sword this is!

LORD.　Is it?

TARO.　Indeed it is.

LORD.　Well, Taro my boy! You did splendidly. By the by, did he say anything?

TARO.　Yes, he did. He said, "Taro, my dear friend! I thought you were true to me. If you must, why didn't you kill me at home in the presence of my wife and dear children?" He lamented most piteously. Indeed, service to a lord is a melancholy thing. Should anything go wrong, well, that is the end of our life.

LORD.　What you say is very true. I fear I did away very hastily with a man who had served me many a year.

TARO.　Does my lord really think so? (*He weeps.*)

LORD.　I, too, am weeping, and I shall never again execute a man. Since no amount of tears can restore the dead to life, let us stop crying. Come, my boy, wipe off your tears.

Alas, the day is fine, but I find no joy in life. To forget this, I wish to pay homage to the good Buddha of Kiyomizu temple. You come with me.

TARO.　Very well, sir.

LORD.　The more I think of it, the more regrettable this affair seems.

TARO.　Indeed it was a regrettable affair.

LORD.　*Yai*, Taro! Is not that Buaku there coming toward us? Quick! Go and see.

TARO.　Alas, this is the Meeting of the Six Ways of Existence, and the disconsolate soul of Buaku, I fear, is walking the earth. I shall go and inquire.

Yai, yai! The lord has seen you now. Why didn't you flee from the capital at once?

BUAKU. Alas, alack! I came here to bid farewell to the Buddha of Kiyomizu. I am again caught in the clutches of cruel fate, and there is no way out. My mind is made up. Kill me at once.

TARO. No, no! Change your appearance right away and come back as a ghost.

BUAKU. I see! Very well. (*He disappears.*)

TARO. Is my lord here? That did look like Buaku, but it evidently was his ghost, for when I followed and called to it, it disappeared.

LORD. *Yai, yai!* Taro boy, look! There it is again.

TARO. That certainly must be his ghost.

BUAKU. Unable to go to Heaven,
Unable to remain on earth,
I wander about at the Meeting of the Six Ways.

TARO. Sir, I have no more doubt about it. That is poor Buaku's ghost.

BUAKU. Oh, please, sir!

TARO. My lord, Buaku is calling to you!

LORD. You go and find out what he wants.

TARO. No, sir! You had better go and find out yourself.

LORD. No, you go.

BUAKU. I am very happy to have met you here. I have a message from your grandfather to deliver to you. Your grandfather says he is greatly embarrassed serving Yama, the king of Hades, day and night, without a sword to wear, and he wishes you to send one by me.

LORD. Indeed, if I were at home, I could present him with the best sword in my possession all wrapped up in the ceremonial style, but here that cannot be. Though this one is slightly worn, I shall be delighted to present it to my honored grandfather.

BUAKU. I will tell him so. He also wishes to have an overcoat, a skirt, and a fan.

LORD. Nothing could be simpler. Taro, help me to get them off. Please tell him that I am exceedingly sorry that they are a little creased and wrinkled, but I am very happy to be of any service to him.

TARO. Well, Buaku! Please deliver these.

BUAKU. Oh, Taro, these were all the things that I was asked to get, but will you tell your lord that I have a message which I must deliver in person?

TARO. Please, my lord! Buaku wishes to speak to you in person.

LORD. *Ha*, what can it be?

BUAKU. Please, my honored lord . . .

LORD. Be quick. What is it?

BUAKU. Your grandfather says that since the terrestrial plane is crowded and full of misery, he wishes me to bring you to a holy and more spacious place. Please come and I will accompany you.

LORD. Well, Buaku, tell my grandfather that I prefer this place though it is sordid and cramped. Perhaps later I may like to come.

BUAKU. But I must take you back with me. I will lead you by hand.

TARO. My lord, it looks as if Buaku may lead you away, willy-nilly. You had better run.

LORD. That is a good idea. Taro, my boy, you come, too.

TARO. Oho! My lord has run away. Look here, Buaku, wasn't that a good piece of work?

BUAKU. Thanks entirely to you. I am greatly obliged to you. This certainly was most unexpected good fortune. Not only was my life spared but also I received farewell gifts.

TARO. You had better make haste and flee from the capital at once.

BUAKU. That I will. Pray see that my family lacks nothing. Farewell! Farewell!

A BAG OF TANGERINES

(Kôji-dawara)

Characters: A TANGERINE DEALER, A FARMER, HIS SON.

DEALER. I am one who lives nearby. Every fall I go about the country buying tangerines, and that's my trade. The seasons change and the time has come for me to make my rounds. I must hasten.

I want to work especially hard this year and make money. Why! I have come so fast that I am already at the gate of a house where I usually can buy good tangerines. I will inquire.

Please, is anyone in?

FARMER. Someone is at the gate. Who is it?

DEALER. It is I.

FARMER. Oh, is it you? I was just thinking it was almost time for you to come around. Have you come to buy tangerines?

DEALER. That's exactly why I have come. Will you sell me some?

FARMER. I was expecting you and have kept some ready.

DEALER. I am greatly obliged to you. If you will put them in a bag, I shall call for them tomorrow.

FARMER. Very well. I shall do so. I am glad you dropped in.

DEALER. Well, I must move on.

SON. What have I heard? Father says that he is going to sell all the tangerines to that dealer, and I am very sorry to hear that. I intended to eat as many as I could while they were on

41

the tree, but I have not got around to them yet. But where are they? I must find them and have a few before they are all gone.

Very good. Here they are! I will open the bag and taste a few. This is really delicious. One is not enough. Just one more! Good! They seem to be especially sweet this year. *Yum, yum!* The more I eat, the more I want.

Alas! What shall I do? I intended to eat only a few, but before I knew it, the bag was entirely empty. What will my father say when he finds this out? I am awfully sorry.

Ha, but I have an idea. Everybody knows that this tangerine dealer is honest but cowardly. Luckily, there hangs a devil's mask on the wall. I will put it on and crawl into the bag. Here I am. This is fine.

DEALER.   Yesterday I bought a bag of tangerines from a farmer. I must go and claim it.

Oh, I have hurried along so that I am already here. Please, is the master in?

FARMER.   I am right here.

DEALER.   I hope the tangerines are in the bag.

FARMER.   They are. Please take them with you.

DEALER.   I am obliged to you. Later I will send some goods in exchange. Well, I shall carry them home. Just help me to lift the bag on my back, will you?

FARMER.   Very well. Is that right?

DEALER.   That's good. I must be going.

FARMER.   Good-bye! Good-bye!

DEALER.   Good-bye.

I was lucky to get these fine tangerines. Now I must hurry home. But what was the matter with me today? Time has gone fast. It is already so dark that I cannot see anything at all. Alas, I have lost my way. There is not a soul who can direct me either. What shall I do?

Oh, here are two roads. Shall I go to the right, or shall I go to the left?

SON. To the right.

DEALER. *Ha!* This is strange. I heard a voice, but in this pitch dark night, there cannot be anyone around. I wonder if it was a fox. I feel utterly helpless. I want to hurry; yet I do not want to lose my way again. Which shall I take, right or left?

SON. Listen! This way, this way! (*He pulls the dealer's right ear.*)

DEALER. Oh, what a misfortune! The tangerines have turned into a man who pulls my ear. Help! Oh, please help me! I shall abandon the bag and run.

SON. I will devour you.

DEALER. How terrible! The tangerines have turned into a devil. Please spare my life.

SON. Eat you up! Eat you up! You shall not get away. I'll devour you in a mouthful.

DEALER. How terrible! Oh, spare my life. Pardon, pardon!

THE FOX MOUND
(*Kitsune-zuka*)

Characters: A LAND-OWNER, TARO and JIRO, *his attendants.*

LAND-OWNER.   I am a land-owner who dwells in this vicinity. I have in my possession a farm which is doing well this year. Unfortunately, however, monkeys and badgers, foxes and deer come nightly and ruin it.   I'll call Taro, my attendant, and send him there.

Yai, yai!   Is Taro around?

TARO.   *Ha!* in your presence.

LAND-OWNER.   It is nothing special that I called you for.   This year until recently my farm has done well, but it has become infested with wild beasts.   I wish you to go there tonight and guard it.   If you see any beasts, drive them away.

TARO.   I obey, but am I to go alone?

LAND-OWNER.   Yes.   Later, however, I will send Jiro.   You go first.

TARO.   Very well.

LAND-OWNER.   By the by, there is a foxes' hole on the hillside. Take care not to be bewitched by them.

TARO.   They are dangerous.   I shall be very careful.   I am leaving now.

LAND-OWNER.   Come back tomorrow morning early.

TARO.   Yes, sir.

LAND-OWNER.   That's all.

TARO.   It is very provoking to have to work day and night. Such is life!

As I have hurried along, I am already at my master's farm. I have to take good care of it.

LAND-OWNER.   I have sent Taro to my farm. He must be getting lonesome.   I will send Jiro now.

Yai, yai! Is Jiro around?

JIRO.   *Ha!* in your presence.

LAND-OWNER.   I am sorry to have to call you so late at night, but will you go to the farm and keep Taro company?

JIRO.   Very well, sir.

LAND-OWNER.   Fill a bamboo flask[1] and take it along.

JIRO.   Thank you, sir.

This is indeed troublesome business, but 'tis my master's command.   There is no way out.

It is very dark tonight, and I do not know where I am.   I think I will call to Taro.

Hoy, hoy! Taro boy, where are you?

TARO.   *Ha!*   Here comes a fox mimicking the voice of Jiro. That is a very good disguise indeed!   I must not get fooled. First I have to wet my eyelashes.

JIRO.   *Hoy, hoy!*

TARO.   *Hoy,* here I am.

JIRO.   Where are you?

TARO.   Right here.   Are you Jiro?

JIRO.   Right you are.   By the master's request I have come to keep you company.

TARO.   I am very happy to see you.   Well, I should say this is very clever.   It looks exactly like Jiro.   I will catch him and bind his hands and feet.

Listen, Jiro boy!   A few minutes ago a big deer came over from yonder hill, and when I chased it, it ran back frightened.

JIRO.   That is very good.

---

[1] A *sake* container.

TARO. Come here! I cannot let you get away.

JIRO. What on earth are you doing to me?

TARO. What on earth indeed! I am not going to be fooled by a silly fox, do you think?

JIRO. But I am Jiro, your fellow servant.

TARO. Indeed you are Jiro all right. Thus tied to a post, you look exceedingly handsome. Oh, Mr. Fox, pretty soon I shall skin you.

LAND-OWNER. I sent Taro and Jiro to my farm, but I have misgivings about them. I will go myself and see how they fare. *Hoy, hoy!* Taro boy and Jiro boy! *Hoy, hoy!*

TARO. What? There comes another fox, and it is mimicking my master's voice. I will catch this one too. *Hoy, hoy!*

LAND-OWNER. *Hoy,* where are you?

TARO. Right here.

LAND-QWNER. Oh, are you there? I thought you might get lonesome, so I came over to see you. I sent Jiro earlier in the evening.

TARO. Jiro boy is right there.
This one, too, has disguised itself very well; indeed it is a living image of my master. I am not going to be fooled, however, by a silly beast.
You rascal! I will catch you.

LAND-OWNER. What in the name of the Holy Buddha are you doing? It is I, your master.

TARO. What in the name of the Holy Buddha indeed! I will bind you tight to this tree and smoke you with pine needles. That should make you show yourself in your true nature. Come, where is your bushy tail? Howl like a good fox, too.

LAND-OWNER. To treat your master like this! You . . .

TARO. What is my noble fox mumbling? I will smoke this one too. Come, howl like a good fox.

JIRO.   Oh, help, help!

TARO.   Look how they wiggle and squirm.
I will bring a sharp sickle and skin both of you. Wait just
a second, you naughty beasts, and I will make an end to all your
follies.

LAND-OWNER.   What a pitiful sight indeed! Poor Taro has
gone stark mad.
Yai, is that you, Jiro?

JIRO.   Indeed it is. Are you my master?

LAND-OWNER.   You are right. Are you bound, too?

JIRO.   I certainly am.

LAND-OWNER.   He said he was going after a sickle to skin us.
Can't you get yourself untied?

JIRO.   I have been trying hard. Now it does look as though
I might be able to get myself free. Ah, I am free! Now I
can help you. What a hateful rascal Taro is! What had we
better do to punish him?

LAND-OWNER.   He won't dare to come near us if he sees us
free, so we had better pretend we are still bound. When he
comes near us, we will seize him.

JIRO.   Excellent! Excellent!

LAND-OWNER.   Get back to the post and pretend . . .

TARO.   Two naughty, naughty foxes! You had better say
your last prayers.

LAND-OWNER.   Come, Jiro!

JIRO.   Right here.

LAND-OWNER.   I've got him. Shake him up and down.

TARO.   Hey, hey! you foxes. What do you think you are doing?

LAND-OWNER.   You call me a fox, you wretch! I've got you
bound. Now how about it?

TARO.   What! Are you really my master and Jiro boy?
Pardon, pardon!

THE LETTER "I"
(*I-moji*)

Characters: A FEUDAL LORD, TARO, *his attendant*, A LADY, A TRAVELLER.

LORD.   Is Taro boy around?

TARO.   In your presence.

LORD.   As you are aware, I have been a bachelor for these many years, but now I have decided to take a spouse. The most merciful Kwannon of Kiyomizu, I hear, is known to be good at match-making. Today I wish to visit her and pray that she will grant me a good wife. You accompany me.

TARO.   I am very happy to hear your decision, for people have been saying that perhaps you, in your previous existence, were either an ox or a horse. To interpret it, they mean you have no settled consort, and I have been greatly mortified to hear it. We will hasten to the temple.

LORD.   Whatever I do or do not do, people will gossip, and you should not take it to heart. Come, we will make haste. (*They start out.*)

TARO.   Oh, my lord! Here is a shrine of Koyasu. Please come and worship!

LORD.   But first I want to go to Kiyomizu. Be quick!

TARO.   You do not understand. This is the shrine for the goddess of child bearing, so do come and pay her homage.

LORD.   That is exceedingly felicitous, but I will worship her on my way back. Come quick! Oh, already we are in front of the shrine. First I will ring the bell. *Ja-gwa-ran! Boom!*

48

Oh, the most merciful Kwannon! Your humble servant has no avowed spouse. Please grant him one!

How holy and how august! *Yai*, Taro, I think I shall hold a vigil here tonight. You stay there, awake, and when the fowl cries, call me.

TARO.   What fowl, my lord?

LORD.   You are a dunce. I mean a barnyard fowl.

TARO.   Will a hen do?

LORD.   You rascal! Wake me when a cock crows. (*He goes to sleep.*)

TARO.   This is awful. My lord who is to hold a vigil is asleep, and here I have to sit up all night. I am getting very lonesome and cannot keep myself awake.

My lord! Oh, my lord!

LORD.   What is the matter? Has the cock crowed?

TARO.   No, sir, but it yawned.

LORD.   You idiot! You do not need to notice its yawn, but wake me when it crows. (*He falls asleep again.*)

TARO.   Well, this is terrible. I am getting sleepy. I shall take a little nap.

LORD.   *Yai, yai!* Taro boy!

TARO.   *Ha!* Did the cock crow?

LORD.   You are incorrigible. Listen! The august Kwannon spoke to me in my dream. She said, "Thy spouse is standing on a stone step of the western gate. Take her to be thy life-mate."

Let us hurry to the western gate.

TARO.   This is indeed very apt. Let us hasten.

LORD.   Look! There she stands. You go and bring her to me.

TARO.   Very well, sir. (*He goes, but comes back.*)

But my lord, you go. I am a bit embarrassed.

LORD.   Why should you be embarrassed?   Bring her here to
me on your back.

TARO.   I obey.
    Oh, my noble lady!   We should welcome you with a litter
or a palanquin, but this time please accept my back.   Pray
get up on my back.   I am the lord's faithful servant, and I
hope I can win your favor too.   Please do get on my back.

LADY.   Should a humble maiden win his favor,
              Come, dear lord, and call on her
           In the far province of Ise
              Under the shadows of the Ise-dera!

TARO.   Never mind about that now.   Let that be your bed-
time story, my lady.   Do get on my back.   (*Exit* LADY.)
    What?   This is strange.   I wonder where she has gone.
    My lord, are you there?

LORD.   Come!   I am anxious to meet her.

TARO.   She is gone that way.   (*He points toward the steps.*)

LORD.   What are you talking about?

TARO.   That's just it.   She was mumbling something and all
of a sudden disappeared.

LORD.   But what did she say?

TARO.   "Should a humble maiden win his favor,
              Come, dear lord, and call on her . . . I . . . I . . ."
    Well, there was something more to it, but I cannot remember.
    I . . . I . . . it was something about "I," but it is gone.

LORD.   Was there much after that?

TARO.   Oh, yes, she said something or other at great length.

LORD.   That sounds like a poem, but what had we better do?
This is very sad.   Ah, now I have hit upon a good scheme.
I will set up a barrier and stop every traveller and try to make
him complete the poem.

TARO.   However, it does seem odd to set up a barrier in this
peaceful imperial reign.

LORD.   I am not going to charge anything, so it will be all right.

TARO.   That may be all right.

LORD.   Then you set up a barrier.   (TARO *stretches a rope across the stage.*)

TRAVELLER.   I am a messenger on very urgent business.   I must make haste.

TARO.   There!   I caught one.

TRAVELLER.   Caught one?   I am neither a bird nor a beast. What is this all about?

TARO.   This is the barrier.

TRAVELLER.   In this peaceful reign, what is the barrier for?

TARO.   We are not going to cross-examine or tax you.

TRAVELLER.   I am glad to hear that.   But what is this for, tell me.

TARO.   That is a rather long story, but listen.   The gentleman who stands there is my master who has been a bachelor for these many years.   He, however, decided to find a spouse, so we came here to ask Kwannon for one.   Luckily Kwannon granted him one, but the lady recited a poem and ran away, and nowhere can she be found.   Now we only know the first half of the poem, and the reason we set up this barrier is to stop the travellers and make them give us the last half of the poem.   Be quick and give us the rest.

TRAVELLER.   Who was it that took the lady's message?

TARO.   None but this clever Taro boy.

TRAVELLER.   If this very clever Taro boy does not know the rest, how can you expect it of a silly traveller like me?   Let me go.

LORD.   Hey, Taro boy!   If he does not give the remaining part of the poem, do not let him go.

TRAVELLER.   How very annoying!   But what was the first part of the poem?

TARO.   "Should a humble maiden win his favor,
                    Come, dear lord, and call on her . . . I . . . I . . ."
        Well, some word beginning with "I" follows soon after, but I
        cannot remember.

TRAVELLER.   Then what followed by necessity must be the
        name of a province that begins with "I." I will name a few
        places, so you see if I am right.

TARO.   Then please name them.

TRAVELLER.   Life is strange! To perform a duty of a match-
        maker to a stranger. Strange indeed!
            Well, a province or a locality that begins with a letter "I"?
        Letter "I"? Was it the province of Iga?

TARO.   Nay, nay, my dear fellow. You are far off.

TRAVELLER.   By the name of Buddha, what could it be?
        "I"? Was it Ise?

TARO.   Good! That's it. Ise, that's right.

LORD.   Recite the poem.

TARO AND LORD.   Should a humble maiden win his favor,
                            Come, dear lord, and call on her
                            In the far province of Ise . . .

TARO.   I am stuck. That is a shame. I am stuck again in
        the very last line.

TRAVELLER.   Whether you get stuck at the last or in the
        beginning, that's no concern of mine. Let me go through
        here. I am on a very urgent errand. Let the next person
        who passes here, finish it for you.

TARO.   Willy-nilly, I must make you complete the poem.

TRAVELLER.   This is most exasperating. A province, by
        necessity, must have a village. I shall name a few villages
        that begin with the letter "I." You see if I am right.

TARO.   You are indeed very clever and resourceful. Please
        name them.

TRAVELLER.   "I," "I?" Well, how about the village of Ikoma?

TARO.   Nay, nay, my dear fellow! I fear you are very far off.

TRAVELLER.   By the miracle of our Amidha Buddha! It might be the village of Ise-dera.

TARO.   That's it. That's it.

LORD.   Recite the entire poem.

LORD AND TARO.   Should a humble maiden win his favor,
            Come, dear lord, and call on her
        In the far province of Ise
            Under the shadow of the Ise-dera!

TRAVELLER.   Fare you well,
        Thou, barrier-keeper:
    Fare you well.

LORD AND TARO.   Alas, we are loath to part with you!

TRAVELLER.   I too am unwilling to part, but look, the sun has . . .

LORD AND TARO.   Already gone down below the horizon.

THREE TOGETHER.   Then fare thee well!
        Though the plum petals fade and fall,
        The pine needles remain
            Forever and ever green on the branch . . .

(Music and dance)

THE MAGIC MALLET OF THE DEVIL
(*Oni no Tsuchi*)

Characters: THE DEVIL, *from the Horai no Shima*, JIMBEI, GOHEI, CHORUS.

DEVIL.   Dressed in the invisible hat and cloak! The magic mallet in my hand is the priceless treasure.

I am a devil from the *Horai no Shima*, Island of Eternal Youth. In this peaceful imperial reign, I hear the fair of the Dragon's Day in Japan is very flourishing. Now I wish to cross over to the land of Japan to purchase the necessary articles.

Peace reigns over all.
Waves of His beneficence
Know no bounds.
With my heart burning with zeal,
I hasten along, passing
The Land of the Reedy Plain, known only in name,
Till at last I reach the Land of the Rising Sun.
Indeed as I hasten along I am already in the Isles of Japan.

I have come so long a distance that I am weary. First I shall sit here and rest a while.

JIMBEI.   Is Mr. Gohei in?

GOHEI.   I am here.

JIMBEI.   Today is the fair of the Dragon's Day, so I wish to go and purchase a few things. What do you think?

GOHEI.   That is an excellent idea.

JIMBEI.   Oh, I see you brought a flask of *sake*.

GOHEI.   Yes, I thought I had better take a small bottle along.

JIMBEI.   I will carry it.   Give it to me.

GOHEI.   Oh, no, that's all right.   Now let us go.

JIMBEI.   Then let us go.   Come, come!

GOHEI.   Very well.

JIMBEI.   In a place like a fair, unless we have a little something, it is not at all interesting.

GOHEI.   You are right.   As you say with a little *sake* inside us, then everything looks good and amusing.

JIMBEI.   Let's go all around the fair and get what we want.

GOHEI.   All right.   Let's!

DEVIL.   Um-m!   *Ha*, I smell a man.   A human being must be coming along.   If I can induce him to be my travelling companion, it will be very good.
    Yai, yai!   Who goes there?

JIMBEI.   *Ha*, some one is calling us.

GOHEI.   Indeed some one has called.

JIMBEI.   Who is it that called to us?

DEVIL.   *Yai, yai!*   I am right here.

JIMBEI.   But who is it?   Though I hear your august voice, I cannot see your noble presence.

GOHEI.   Indeed where could he be?   I cannot see him either.

DEVIL.   *Ha*, I know.   With this hat and cloak, it may be that men of Japan cannot see me.   I will slip them off.

JIMBEI.   Strange!   What do you think of this?   There is the voice right in front of us; yet we cannot see the presence. This is very mysterious.

GOHEI.   This is the trick of a fox or a badger.   It is teasing us.

DEVIL.   Here, here!   Look!   I am right here.

JIMBEI AND GOHEI.   Where, may we ask?

DEVIL.   Right here!   (*He stamps his feet.*)

JIMBEI AND GOHEI.   Oh, terrible, terrible! Please spare our lives, I beg you!

DEVIL.   Come, come, my dear fellows! I am not so terrible. I am a devil from the Island of Eternal Youth.

JIMBEI.   But if the devil is not frightening, what is?

GOHEI AND JIMBEI.   Please spare our lives!

DEVIL.   Do not be so anxious! The gods do no injustice, so the proverb says. I shall not do anything to you. Rest assured.

JIMBEI AND GOHEI.   We thought you might eat us up in a mouthful.

DEVIL.   Oh, no! Certainly not. I am not the kind that eats such a foul thing as a man. Do not worry!

JIMBEI AND GOHEI.   We are greatly relieved to hear it.

DEVIL.   By the by, where are you going?

JIMBEI AND GOHEI.   We live in this neighborhood, but as there is the fair of the Dragon's Day in town, we are on our way there.

DEVIL.   This devil, too, came from the Island of Eternal Youth to attend the fair. This is a very happy meeting. I will accompany you.

JIMBEI AND GOHEI.   We shall be very happy to keep you company.

DEVIL.   Come! One of you go first as a guide.

JIMBEI.   This is strange. I hear the voice, but I cannot see him. Where are you?

DEVIL.   Look! I am right here.

GOHEI AND JIMBEI.   Wherever you are, we see nothing.

DEVIL.   Oh, yes, (*aside*) I remember! I shall take the hat and cloak off again.

JIMBEI.   This is very strange.

GOHEI.   As you say, it is very mysterious.

DEVIL.   Here, here I am.

JIMBEI.   Oh, were you there?   But you appear and disappear, and we cannot understand it at all.   I wish you would explain to us the reason.

DEVIL.   It is no wonder you are mystified.   I will tell you. These are treasures called the invisible hat and cloak.   With them on no human being can see us.   Hence they are valuable treasures.

JIMBEI.   Then are these the famous invisible hat and cloak of which we have heard so much?

DEVIL.   As you say, they are.

JIMBEI.   Indeed I am very thankful to have this opportunity of seeing the priceless treasure of the foreign land.

DEVIL.   You ought to be.

JIMBEI.   By the by, I hear there is another treasure known as a wonder mallet.   Could you tell me what it is like?

DEVIL (*aside*).   He begins to question me on a serious matter, but while I am about it, I might as well tell him.

Listen! This treasure mallet is the most valuable of the three, and whenever you shake it, anything you wish comes out.   I wear it always next to my skin.

JIMBEI.   Naturally!

DEVIL.   For a long while I have been looking at what you have in your hand.   What is it?

GOHEI.   This is a little flask.

DEVIL.   What is a flask?

JIMBEI.   It is a *sake* container.

DEVIL.   What? *Sake?*

GOHEI.   Indeed it is!

DEVIL.   Can't you treat me to a cup?

GOHEI.   Luckily I have been longing for it, so let us have a drink.

JIMBEI.   Good!   Come, open the flask.

GOHEI.   Very well.

JIMBEI.   First won't you sit down?

DEVIL.   All right.

GOHEI.   I have opened it.   First to Sir Devil!

DEVIL.   No, you begin first.

JIMBEI.   No, you first.

DEVIL.   All right then.   I will play the rôle of host and pour
for you.

GOHEI.   'Tis impolite to make you work.   I will serve you first.

DEVIL.   I am obliged to you.   We will all have some now.

GOHEI.   Thank you.   Now I will pour for you.

JIMBEI.   My turn now.

GOHEI.   Well, well!   I am getting very joyous.

JIMBEI.   How about a little song?

GOHEI.   All right.

> A faithful friendship
> Is a treasure, a treasure
> Bought at the fair . . .

DEVIL.   Truly, this is cool and exceedingly delicious!

JIMBEI.   Sir Devil has finished his first.   Do have more.

GOHEI.   Oh, you must keep on.   Do have some more.

DEVIL.   But first you had better have some, too.

GOHEI.   We will.   So have more.

DEVIL.   Well then.   Another cup!

GOHEI.   That's good.   (*He sings again.*)

DEVIL.   That is very interesting.
    I can't quaff this cup in one breath.   I will set it down a
minute.

JIMBEI.   That is all right.

DEVIL.   I hear that men in the Isles of Japan sing and dance
to entertain themselves.   How about a dance now?

GOHEI.   Oh, no! I am sorry. I am not at all good at that.

DEVIL.   Come, come! I think you are. It is my special desire to see you perform.

GOHEI.   If that is the case, I will. Please hum the music.

JIMBEI.   Very well. (*He dances.*)

DEVIL.   Splendid! It is worthy of a Japanese dance. So gracious and entertaining!

JIMBEI.   This dance will serve to improve the *sake*. Have another cup!

DEVIL.   Gladly.

GOHEI.   I will have one too.

DEVIL.   Oh, come! I will offer you my cup!

GOHEI.   Thank you so much.

DEVIL.   Here, one for you! Take it.

GOHEI.   Thank you. Now I wish Sir Devil would give us a dance. What do you think? You ask him.

JIMBEI.   Pardon me. I hesitate to ask you, but we should be delighted if you could give us a performance.

DEVIL.   I wish I could entertain you, but the dance of the Island of Eternal Youth is not interesting.

JIMBEI.   You are too modest. It will be very interesting, and I wish you would.

DEVIL.   If that is the case, then I will dance a little. (DEVIL *dances.*)

JIMBEI AND GOHEI.   Splendid! Splendid!

JIMBEI.   It was uncommonly entertaining.

GOHEI.   That certainly was a pretty show!

DEVIL.   Not at all.

JIMBEI.   Have another cup!

GOHEI.   Yes, please do.

JIMBEI.   Here! This one to Sir Devil.

DEVIL.   Aren't you through with *sake* yet?

JIMBEI.   A few minutes ago you gave me a cup.   Now I wish
to return it.

DEVIL.   Well, then.   This is an enormous cup.   If I take it
in one gulp, I shall get dead drunk.

GOHEI.   I don't think so.

DEVIL.   There it goes.   (GOHEI *gets up and sings.*)

DEVIL.   I can't quite down it all.   (*To* JIMBEI)
Now you dance.

JIMBEI.   Please excuse me.

DEVIL.   Come, come!   Three gods with their due arts, so the
proverb says.   You get up and dance for us now.

JIMBEI.   Very well.   Please intone the music.

GOHEI.   All right.   (JIMBEI *dances.*)

DEVIL.   Excellent!   Very well done!   That was uncommonly
pretty.   I will give you this invisible hat as a token of my
appreciation.

JIMBEI.   I am greatly obliged to you for granting me this desire
not yet expressed.

DEVIL.   This invisible cloak to you for your lovely songs.

GOHEI.   This is indeed an unexpected good fortune.

DEVIL.   I will just finish up this cup.   So you put away the
rest.

JIMBEI.   Won't you have just a very little?

DEVIL.   No more, no more!   Put it away quickly.

GOHEI.   Then I will put it away.

DEVIL.   Let us hurry to the fair of the Dragon's Day.

JIMBEI AND GOHEI.   Very well.

DEVIL.   I fear I am a bit tipsy.   Please lead me by the hand.

JIMBEI.   I will lead you.

GOHEI.   I, too, will lead you.

DEVIL. *Ha, ha!* I see eight or nine paths in front of me. *Ha, ha!*

JIMBEI AND GOHEI. We have no doubt.

JIMBEI. You are only a little indisposed.

GOHEI. You seem to be so.

DEVIL. How frightening! Terrible, terrible!

JIMBEI. What is the matter, may I ask?

DEVIL. Yonder between the two stone buildings, a branch of holly [1] is coming out right into the path. I am scared! *Ha, ha, ha!*

JIMBEI. You must not be so cowardly. As long as we are with you, you are absolutely safe.

DEVIL. I am exceedingly tipsy. I do not think I can go any farther. I will take a nap here first.

JIMBEI. That will be good.

DEVIL. Then I will sleep a little.

JIMBEI. I will rub your back a little.

GOHEI. I will rub your arms.

JIMBEI. Well, how do you feel now?

GOHEI. Have we done enough? How is it?

JIMBEI. Oh, please! Please, sir!

GOHEI. How is it?

JIMBEI. Come this way, my friend.

GOHEI. What is the matter?

JIMBEI. This has been a ghastly experience.

GOHEI. Indeed it has.

JIMBEI. Nevertheless we have an unheard-of treasure, which is most fortunate.

---

[1] Holly was considered an effective means of frightening away the devils and was used for the New Year's decoration.

GOHEI. I believe I shall hurry home and show it to my wife and children.

JIMBEI. Wait a moment.

GOHEI. What is the matter?

JIMBEI. As the devil told us, of the three treasures, the magic mallet is the most valuable, and he is wearing it close to his body. How about getting it from him?

GOHEI. Very good, but isn't that a bit terrifying?

JIMBEI. I will go behind and rub his back. You watch your chance and get it from him.

GOHEI. I will try.

JIMBEI. Do not make a mistake.

GOHEI. I will be careful.

JIMBEI. How is my honored devil? I will rub your back.

GOHEI. I will rub your arms.

JIMBEI. How is it, my colleague? Are you coming all right?

GOHEI. Come this way, please.

JIMBEI. What is the matter?

GOHEI. Look, I got it!

JIMBEI. That is splendid. It does look wonderful. Please show it to me.

GOHEI. This is indeed very wonderful. I must hurry home and try to beat out all sorts of treasures.

JIMBEI. But wait a moment!

GOHEI. What is the matter now?

JIMBEI. Give that mallet to me.

GOHEI. Oh, no! I took it from the devil. Why should I give it to you?

JIMBEI. What? You are an unreasonable fellow. I suggested it first, and it belongs to me. Give it to me. I must have it.

GOHEI.　No, sir! I risked my life for it. I can't give it to you.

BOTH.　Give it to me. This way, no, this way . . .

DEVIL.　Hum-um! What is this fuss about? What noisy fellows you are! What? Isn't that my magic mallet?

BOTH.　We are very sorry.

DEVIL.　Ah, what ungrateful wretches you both are! If you are so wicked, no amount of shaking the mallet will bring anything. I will use my good judgment and give you your wishes. First give it to me.

JIMBEL.　Very well, sir.

DEVIL.　I wish to be impartial. So instead of giving one of you the mallet, I will grant wealth and health as well as all kinds of treasures from this mallet to you and your descendants.

BOTH.　Oh, thank you very much!

DEVIL.　Come, I will give you treasures.

CHORUS.　So saying, the devil shook the magic mallet, and — lo and behold! — gold and silver, jewels and precious stones, rice, and all sorts of food bubbled out. The two men of the Isles of Japan gratefully received them and went on their way, happy and light-hearted. The devil, too, with his mallet on his shoulder, bade farewell to the Isles of the Rising Sun and returned to the Island of Eternal Youth.

GARGOYLE

(*Oni-gawara*)

Characters: A COUNTRY GENTLEMAN, TARO, *his attendant.*

GENTLEMAN.   I am an inhabitant of the distant country.   I must call my attendant and speak with him.
  Is Taro boy around?

TARO.   Coming!

GENTLEMAN.   Where are you?

TARO.   Right here.

GENTLEMAN.   It is nothing very special that I want you for. But I have been staying in the capital for a long while, and as I am getting a little weary, I wish to take a stroll.   What do you think of the idea?

TARO.   It is a splendid idea.   You have not been out for a long while.

GENTLEMAN.   Then let us go.

TARO.   Very well, sir.

GENTLEMAN.   What do you think?   To me this kind of impromptu expedition is much pleasanter than a long well-planned one.

TARO.   Very true, indeed.   Though you have many good friends who would be glad of your company, you seem to enjoy being free to walk at random with your humble servant.

GENTLEMAN.   Quite right.   I prefer having you alone to being surrounded by uncongenial people.   I feel at home.

TARO.   You are very kind.

GENTLEMAN.   Oh, here is a great hall.   Do you know what it is?

TARO.   Do you not know what it is?

GENTLEMAN.   I do not.

TARO.   Why, this is the famous Rokkaku Hall of the imperial capital.

GENTLEMAN.   Yes, I have heard of such a hall. So this is the merciful Kwannon of the Rokkaku Hall!

TARO.   Indeed it is.

GENTLEMAN.   True to its fame, it is a wonderful temple.

TARO.   It is.

GENTLEMAN.   Let us pay homage to Kwannon.

TARO.   Very well, sir.

GENTLEMAN.   Thou merciful Kwannon! May good fortune ever smile on my country and my people. Grant us wealth and health and long life.

   Now let us go to the hall in the rear.

TARO.   Very well, sir.

GENTLEMAN.   Come! Follow me.

TARO.   I am following.

GENTLEMAN.   Look at this votive tablet. It is worthy of the great imperial capital. A wonderful drawing.

   Oh, high up on the roof, I see something fearful. What is that?

TARO.   That is called a gargoyle or a grotesque.

GENTLEMAN.   What a fiendish face it has!

TARO.   It certainly is fiendish.

GENTLEMAN.   Wait a moment. That face reminds me of some one I know well. Can you recall who it is?

TARO.   I am afraid not. I do not believe there could be any one in the wide world who resembles that monster.

GENTLEMAN.   Yes, I am certain I know some one who looks exactly like that. Hum, hum! Boo-hoo, boo-hoo!

TARO.   Pardon me, but what makes you so sorrowful?

GENTLEMAN.   Taro, my boy, it is no wonder that you are vexed to see me weep thus.   For a moment I could not recall the person who is the very image of that gargoyle, but now I know.   It is my wife whom I left in my native country.   I became homesick for her all of a sudden.

TARO.   Indeed, come to think of it, it is her very image.

GENTLEMAN.   When she flies up in a temper, she looks exactly like that.

TARO.   Very true, sir.

GENTLEMAN.   When she is in a good humor, she smiles just like that.

TARO.   Ah, sir!   There you are a bit partial.   Your wife has as big a mouth as our kitchen stew-pan.

GENTLEMAN.   But alas!   I am ashamed to think I have such a wife.

TARO.   Oh, no!   You should not take that too much to heart.

GENTLEMAN.   Well, Taro boy!   I was a fool to get so wrought up over my homely wife in the country.   Though I cannot care for her, she has given me many marvelous sons who are my wealth and future hope.   That is wondrously lucky for me.

TARO.   Indeed it is.

GENTLEMAN.   Well, then let us go home laughing and rejoicing.

TARO.   Very good, sir.

GENTLEMAN.   Come, you laugh first.

TARO.   No, sir!   Please, you first.

BOTH.   *Ha, ha, ha, a-ha!   A-ha, ha, ha!*

THE BIRD–CATCHER IN HADES
(*Esashi Jûwô*)

Characters: YAMA, *the king of Hades,* KIYOYORI, *a bird-catcher,*
DEMONS, CHORUS.

YAMA.　　Yama the king of Hades, Yama the king of Hades,
comes to the Meeting of the Six Ways.

　　Yai, yai!　Are my satellites around?

DEMONS.　　*Ha!*　Here we are.

YAMA.　　If any sinners come along, drive them into Hell.

DEMONS.　　We certainly will.

KIYOYORI.　　All men are sinners, and I am no more a sinner
than the rest of them.

　　My name is Kiyoyori, a bird-catcher, who was well known
in the terrestrial plane.　But my life-span, like all things in the
vale of tears, came to its end, and I was caught by the wind of
impermanence.　Now I am on the way to the world of dark-
ness.

　　Without a pang of parting,
　　Without a tinge of remorse,
　　I forsake the world of impermanence,
　　And as I wander about with no guide,
　　I have already come to the Meeting of the Six Ways.

Indeed, this is already the Meeting of the Six Ways of Existence.　After due consideration, I wish to go to Heaven.

DEMONS.　　*Ha!　Ho!*　We smell a man.　Why, no wonder!
Here comes a sinner.　We will report to Yama.

　　Oh, please, sir!　Here comes the first sinner.

YAMA.　　Make haste and drive him into Hell.

DEMONS.   Very well, sir.

Come, you sinner! Hell is ever at hand, but one cannot say that about Heaven. Make haste. (*A demon takes hold of* KIYOYORI, *who resists violently.*)

Yai, yai! You are different from most of the sinners of the earth. What was your profession on the terrestrial plane?

KIYOYORI.   I was Kiyoyori, the famous bird-catcher.

FIRST DEMON.   Bird-catcher? Taking life from morning till night! Your sins are unfathomably great. I must send you to Hell at once.

KIYOYORI.   Oh, no! I am not such a bad sinner as you make me out to be. Please let me go to Heaven.

FIRST DEMON.   No, that cannot be! But first I shall ask the King about your case.

Pardon, sir!

YAMA.   Well, what is it?

FIRST DEMON.   The sinner who has just arrived says that he was a very famous bird-catcher on the terrestrial plane. So I told him that having taken life day and night, he committed deep sin and certainly is doomed to Hell. But he protests and says that we misjudge him thoroughly. What shall we do about him?

YAMA.   Call the sinner to me.

FIRST DEMON.   Very well.

Come along this way. King Yama wishes to see you.

KIYOYORI.   I am coming.

FIRST DEMON.   Here is that sinner you sent for.

YAMA.   Come, you sinner! You have been sinning all through your life snaring birds, and you are indeed a very wicked man. I am going to send you to Hell at once.

KIYOYORI.   What you say about me is very true, but the birds I caught were used to feed the falcons. There was really no serious harm in that.

YAMA. A falcon is another kind of bird, isn't it?

KIYOYORI. Yes, indeed.

YAMA. Well, then! That puts the case on a slightly different basis. I do not consider that a serious offense.

KIYOYORI. I am glad you don't. It really was more the falcon's fault than mine. That being the case, I hope you will send me straight to Heaven.

YAMA. Since I, the mighty king of Hades, have not yet tasted a bird, catch one with your pole, and let me taste it right here. Then I will grant your wish without further ado.

KIYOYORI. Nothing could be simpler. I shall catch a few birds and present them to you.

CHORUS. To the bird-hunt, bird-hunt!
All at once from the southern paths of the mountain of death,
Many birds come flocking.
Swifter than a flash
The bird-catcher darts and
Snares many with his pole.

KIYOYORI. I will roast them for you. Here, they are ready. Please try one.

YAMA. Well, well! I will have a taste.
Meri, meri! Yum, yum!
Oh, this is uncommonly delicious.

KIYOYORI (*to the demons*). You would like to try them too?

DEMONS. Indeed, we shall!
Meri, meri! Yum, yum!
What marvelous flavor!

YAMA. I have never tasted anything so wonderful. Since you have given us such a treat, I am going to send you back to the terrestrial plane. There you may catch birds for another three years.

KIYOYORI. I am greatly obliged to you, I am sure.

CHORUS.　　　For another three years, you shall snare birds!
　　　　　　Pheasant, goose, peacock, stork, and many others.
　　Thus commanded, Kiyoyori has turned his step once more
to the world beneath. But Yama, loath to see him depart,
bestows on Kiyoyori a jewelled crown. Our bird-catcher
marches lightly to the world below, there to begin his second
span of life.

THE MELON THIEF
(*Uri Nusubito*)

Characters: A COUNTRY GENTLEMAN, A MELON THIEF.

GENTLEMAN.   I am a country gentleman who dwells in this neighborhood.   I have many farms, and as I have not visited them for several days, I shall now do so.   The day is fine, and I shall stroll along.

Though many a man has plenty of farms, people always tell me that nowhere do things grow every year so well as in mine.   Oh, I have come so fast that here I am already at my farm.   How marvelously things have grown since I was here last!   The melons, too, are tinged with beautiful color.   Before birds and beasts get them, I will put up a fence and a scarecrow. Here they are!   That's fine.   I will come again tomorrow.

MELON THIEF.   I live in this vicinity.   Tonight I am invited to a friend's.   Although his house is very far from here and I dislike to travel country roads alone at night, I could not very well refuse since he so kindly sent a messenger and insisted upon my presence this evening.   Perhaps the company is waiting for me already.   I must make haste.

Ha, here is a fence which looks unfamiliar.   What kind of farm is this?   I shall take a look.

Well, well, this is a melon farm.   How fragrant are the ripened melons!   This certainly is an unexpected fortune. Although I wish to pick one or two and make a present to my host, what had I better do?   Luckily the sun has set.   First I will tear down the fence.

Meri, meri!   Kasa, kasa!   Meri, meri!

What a noise!   I wonder if some one heard me.   He certainly will catch me, but I trust no one has.

71

Ha, ha! How absurd. I am covering my mouth in the thought of some one accusing me. Anyway no one heard me, that I am certain. Now I go over the fence.

Oh, so many melons! Which shall I pick? Here! Oh, that's a dead leaf. There! Another dead leaf! What is the matter with me? I cannot understand this. By the by, I was once told that when we pick melons at night, it is best to hunt them lying down.

Ha, here it is! Indeed this is a beauty.

Oh, oh! Please pardon me. I am not a melon thief. I merely lost my way in the dark and somehow wandered into this farm. I have no evil intentions. Oh, please do not keep such absolute silence. It makes me feel so guilty and frightened. Tell me at once that you will forgive me. Oh, please say something. I implore you, folding my already seven-folded knees into eight-fold. Do forgive this poor blunderer.

What? Am I in my right mind? I thought it a man. To think I was entreating on bended knees to a scarecrow! This is very provoking. Why didn't you tell me that you are a scarecrow? What a hateful thing you are! I will knock you down and trample on you. There! I feel better. I will tear up the vines too. There!

Well, my friend must be waiting for me. I have already wasted a great deal of time. I must hasten.

GENTLEMAN. Again I am here at my farm. What is this? Some one has broken through the fence. I cannot understand this. The vines are torn and trampled, and the scarecrow is down. This is not the doing of a bird or a beast, but of a melon thief. This certainly puts me thoroughly out of temper. I must catch him.

Ah, I have an idea. A thief is bound to come back; therefore I am going to stand here as a scarecrow and catch him. I am not going to let him get away this time. So, so! That's good.

MELON THIEF. I am on my way back. Last evening my host praised the melons very highly. He had never before tasted such fruit, he told me. I believe I will take a few home for my family.

Oh, I am here already at the melon farm. The master evidently has not come yet, for I see the fence is still down and the vines trampled and torn as I left them. But this is strange. He must have come, for the scarecrow is up.

Hey, you impudent thing! Did you get up yourself? Listen! You are an incorrigible fellow, but you are so wonderfully made that you look exactly like a human being. That reminds me. The host told me that at the next gathering we may play a game of the demon of Hell torturing sinners. I may be assigned to the part of the demon. I am going to pretend that this scarecrow is a sinner and I a demon. I will torture him. Isn't there a stick around? How lucky! Here is a bamboo stick, the demon's iron rod.

Now the torture of Hell begins.

Hey, hey! You sinner, walk faster, faster! *Ha, ha!* Since he is a scarecrow, no amount of hard torture is going to affect him.

Since the various rôles are to be given out by lots, naturally I may have to play the rôle of a sinner, and he the demon. Now I will try.

"Alas, how wretched! Sad is the fate of a sinner who has just come to Hades. Do not torture me so. I renounce myself before you. Indeed my coming here was foreordained in my previous existence. Torture me no more.

"I would fain escape, but you withhold me;
I would fain stay, but you lash me."

Good gracious! With the phrase "you lash me," he actually lashed me. Ouch, I am sore, and I cannot understand it. Maybe it was just a gust of wind.

It sways and sways. When I push it, it nods its head, and when I pull, lifts it. Pulling and pushing, pushing and pulling

. . . *Ha, ha*, no wonder it lashed me, this marvelous scarecrow! I will make it torture me again.

"I would fain escape, but you withhold me;
I would fain stay, but . . ."

GENTLEMAN. You confounded rascal! I will not let you get away this time.

MELON THIEF. Great Buddha! Help, help! I am tricked. Forgive me, forgive me.

GENTLEMAN. Never, never! You hateful rascal, you stole my melons. Oh, he is running away. Is there no one here? Catch him, catch him. Do not let him get away.

MR. DUMBTARO

(*Dontaro* [1])

Characters: MR. DUMBTARO, HIS LADY OF DOWNTOWN, HIS LADY OF UPTOWN.

DUMBTARO.　　My name is Dumbtaro.　I was a resident of the capital, but I met reverses of fortune and was forced to leave there three years ago, to wander far and wide.　Fickle fortune, however, has not smiled upon me yet.　Nevertheless, I am getting very homesick and wish to return home.　I must hasten.

By the by, though it is not in keeping with my circumstances, I have two establishments, one uptown and the other downtown.　Since I have not written to either of them for three years, I have certain misgivings, but I will call on them.　I hope there is nothing the matter with them.

Oh, as I amble along, here I am already in the capital. Shall I stop to see the Lady of Uptown first?　No.　I will call on the Lady of Downtown, since she lives on my way.　Though I have had no news, I do hope all is well with her.

Here is her house.　How strange!　The sun is not down yet, but her door is closed.　Perhaps it is merely to be cautious. I shall ask.

Hello!　Please open the door.

LADY OF DOWNTOWN.　　Who is it?

DUMBTARO.　　Mr. Dumbtaro has come home, so please open the door.

LADY D.　　Mr. Dumbtaro left for a distant country three years ago, and I have not heard from him since.　As a woman cannot live alone forever, I have taken a cudgel-player for my

[1] The Japanese title *Dontaro* means "Dumb boy."

75

husband. If you do anything rash, you will soon find out
that you have made a mistake.

DUMBTARO. What? What? Took a cudgel-player for a
husband?

LADY D. So I did.

DUMBTARO. You unfaithful wretch! To take a cudgel-player
for a husband without my leave! That is unpardonable. I
will trample down this door and show you what I think of such
a woman. Open the door. Open it.

LADY D. How angry he is! Oh, please, my dear husband,
are you there? Do get your cudgel and knock down this
ruffian at the door. Quick, quick!

DUMBTARO. What is this? Did she really take a cudgel-
player for a husband? I hear the flourishing of a cudgel along
with the wailing of the woman. How provoking this is!

Listen, woman! I am not at all sorry to hear that you have
taken a cudgel-player as your husband. I call that my good
luck. So far as you are concerned, the cooling December gale
has been blowing in my heart already. I have not even a
particle of regret. Now I will go to my Lady of Uptown. I
must hurry.

Indeed, my Lady of Uptown, unlike this faithless wench,
has always been affectionate and sweet. She must be waiting
for me patiently.

Ah, here I am. Her door, too, is closed. Of course! the
sun has already gone down. I will inquire.

Pardon, please open here.

LADY OF UPTOWN. Who is this that asks to open the door?

DUMBTARO. This, my dear, is Mr. Dumbtaro, who has just
come back from a distant country.

Please open the door!

LADY U. Oh, no, you cannot be my Mr. Dumbtaro. You are
a young man of the neighborhood who comes to tease me.

DUMBTARO. Don't you recognize my voice? Truly, this is your Dumbtaro who has come back with his fortune restored. Come, Sweet, open this door quickly!

LADY U. My master Dumbtaro went away to a distant country three years ago, and I have not heard from him at all. Since a woman cannot forever live all alone, I have taken a halberd-player for a husband. If you think circumstances have not changed, you are greatly mistaken.

DUMBTARO. Oh, come, do not lie to me. Open this door quickly.

LADY U. Don't be so silly! Why should I lie about such a matter? If you do anything hasty, you will get hurt.

DUMBTARO. Did you really take a halberd-player for a husband?

LADY U. Why should I lie about it? It is the truth.

DUMBTARO. Is it a fact?

LADY U. It is.

DUMBTARO. Are you telling me this in your right mind?

LADY U. I am in my right mind.

DUMBTARO. Well, well, I am indeed bewitched! You unfaithful wench! I will not let you do such an outlandish thing while the breath is still left in me! Open here! If you don't I will break in through this door and show you what I think of such a wretch. Open here!

LADY U. Oh, how angry he is! Are you there, my dear husband? Please come here and knock him down with your halberd.

DUMBTARO. This is dreadful. She did really take a halberd-player for a husband! I hear the rustling of the halberd together with the woman's screaming.

Listen, you faithless woman! How did you dare to take a husband without my permission? You are indeed an abominable creature. Remember, for I will not let this thing pass without revenge.

Well, this is most distressing to me.　I thought even if the shrew of Downtown might be fickle, my Lady of Uptown would be faithful to me, but I am sadly mistaken about her.　The old proverb says, "Do not trust a woman even if she be the mother of seven children."　How true that is!

Since I have been forsaken by my women, I have no more desire to continue this wretched existence.　I will throw myself in a river or over a waterfall and commit suicide.　But wait a moment!　That's no good.　Suppose people say that Mr. Dumbtaro came back from a distant country, and when he found that his women had forsaken him, he drowned himself.　That will be exceedingly mortifying to my sense of honor.　The only thing now left for me to do is to live and make these women regret what they did.　What had I better do?

Oh, I have an idea.　I shall shave my head and enter into the priesthood.　That is the way to have revenge on them.

Thou august god of Hachiman, be my witness!　This very day Dumbtaro is going into the Koya Monastery.　But I am so very miserable that I can't keep back my tears!　*Boo hoo! Boo hoo!*　(*Exit.*)

LADY D.　　I am Mr. Dumbtaro's Lady of Downtown.　Last night Mr. Dumbtaro came and said that he had come back from a distant country, but as he had not written to me for so very long, I was angry and told him that I had taken a cudgel-player for a husband.　He was enraged and went away saying that he was going to visit his Lady of Uptown.　I am going after him.

As I have not visited the Lady of Uptown, I am a little shy about going there, but I am so anxious to see Mr. Dumbtaro that I must go.

Oh, here I am already.　First I must inquire.　Please, is anyone in?

LADY U.　　How strange!　There is someone at the gate whose voice I do not recognize!

LADY D.   It is I.

LADY U.   I do not believe I have ever seen you before.   Please tell me who you are.

LADY D.   I am Mr. Dumbtaro's Lady of Downtown.

LADY U.   How do you do?   I am very happy to meet you.

LADY D.   As to my present visit, it is nothing very special.   Last night Mr. Dumbtaro came to my door, but as he had not written to me since he left three years ago, I was greatly put out and told him that as a woman could not be alone forever, I had taken a cudgel-player for a husband.   Then he became exceedingly angry and said that he was going to visit his Lady of Uptown and went away.   Please let me see him a few minutes.

LADY U.   Well, as to that, I must tell you my story.   Last night Mr. Dumbtaro came here also, but I thought as usual it was a young man of this neighborhood that was teasing me. So I said that a woman could not very well live alone forever and that I took a halberd-player for a husband; then he became angry and went away.   I am sorry he is not here.

LADY D.   You see how humiliating it is to have to come to you.   So please do not lie to me, but let me see him just a few minutes.

LADY U.   Why should I lie to you?   That is the fact.

LADY D.   Then is it really the truth?

LADY U.   It is really the truth.

LADY D.   Then where do you think he has gone?

LADY U.   I was told by someone that he had gone to the Koya Monastery to be a priest.

LADY D.   Did he really go to the Koya Monastery?

LADY U.   So I was told.

LADY D.   How very sad that is!   What do you think we had better do?

LADY U.   Indeed what had we better do?   Please find a way out of this misery.

LADY D.   I believe if we go to the public highway and wait for him, we may be able to catch him.   Then we can persuade Mr. Dumbtaro to give up this very odious idea of going into the priesthood.

LADY U.   That indeed is an excellent scheme.   I will accompany you.

LADY D.   Then let us go at once.

LADY U.   Please lead the way.

LADY D.   Let us hurry to the highway.

LADY U.   Very well.

LADY D.   If both of us unite thus and beg him to give up the idea of going to the Koya Monastery, I am certain even the very stubborn Mr. Dumbtaro may change his mind.

LADY U.   As you say, when we both beg him, then perhaps he will turn back.

LADY D.   Here we are on the highway.

LADY U.   So we are.

LADY D.   Let us wait for him here.

LADY U.   Very well.

DUMBTARO.   Oh, thou merciful Amidha Buddha, Amidha Buddha!   Dumbtaro of yesterday has gone, and this new Dumbtaro is no more Dumbtaro.   How transitory this world is!   Namu Amidha Buddha!   Amidha Buddha!

LADY D.   Is not that Mr. Dumbtaro who is coming there?

LADY U.   Indeed it is!   You stop him, please.

LADY D.   Very well, I will try.
    If you please, are you not Mr. Dumbtaro?   Oh, how you have changed!   Please give up the idea of going to the Koya Monastery.

DUMBTARO.   Namu Amidha Buddha!   Namu Amidha Buddha!

LADY D.   Oh, please!
    You go and try.

LADY D.   If you please, Mr. Dumbtaro!   What has happened
    to you?

DUMBTARO.   Namu   Amidha   Buddha!   Namu   Amidha
    Buddha!

LADY U.   Let us both try.

LADY D.   Very well.

LADY D. AND LADY U.   Oh, please, Mr. Dumbtaro.   What
    has happened to you?   Please change your mind about going
    into the priesthood.

DUMBTARO.   Why, from the right and from the left, do these
    wicked women call back the noble priest who is on his way to
    the holy monastery of Koya?   Namu Amidha Buddha!

LADY D. AND LADY U.   Your anger is justified, but please give
    up your idea.

DUMBTARO.   Since you have a cudgel-player and a halberd-
    player for husbands, you are not afraid of anyone.   Namu
    Amidha Buddha!   Namu Amidha Buddha!

LADY D. AND LADY U.   Your anger is justified, but now we will
    do everything that you wish us to do, so for this one time, please
    pardon us and give up the idea of going into the priesthood.

DUMBTARO.   Woman's disposition cannot be changed over
    night.   Namu Amidha Buddha!   Namu Amidha Buddha!

LADY D. AND LADY U.   We will promise and swear to Buddha
    that we will obey you in everything.   Please listen to our
    entreaty.

DUMBTARO.   You will do everything that I ask you?

LADY D. AND LADY U.   Indeed, whatever you say.

DUMBTARO.   Then I think out of thirty days of the month, I
    will come and stay with you twenty-five days, Lady of Uptown,
    and the remaining five days with you, Lady of Downtown.

LADY D.   How provoking! That's pure injustice. That cannot be!

DUMBTARO.   Just as I thought! That is the reason I made you
swear and promise, but no use. Namu Amidha Buddha!
Namu Amidha Buddha!

LADY U.   But please wait a moment. Do not be so hasty. I
have a good scheme. Out of thirty days of the month, you
stay fifteen days with each one of us.

DUMBTARO.   You are a clever woman. Then since you live
downtown, I will spend the first half of the month with you,
Lady of Downtown. You, Lady of Uptown, I will spend the
last half of the month with you.

LADY D.   That cannot be, for every other month I lose a day.
That's not fair.

DUMBTARO.   If that cannot be, then Namu Amidha Buddha!
Namu Amidha Buddha!

LADY U.   Oh, my dear Lady of Downtown, please do not be so
exacting. Let such a detail work itself out.

LADY D.   Very well, then. Will you really stay with us?

DUMBTARO.   Promise to do anything and everything I tell you.

LADIES.   Indeed we will.

DUMBTARO.   Then I will give up the idea of the monastery.

LADIES.   Oh, happy, happy day!

DUMBTARO.   Since everybody knows that I decided to go into
the priesthood, we must let them know that you women per-
suaded me to give up the noble idea. Now you both lock your
arms and carry me to your house chanting.

LADIES.   That's very good. But what shall we say?

DUMBTARO.   I say "Whose chariot is this?" Then you chant:
"This is Mr. Dumbtaro's chariot!" Put "Sir" in front of my
name. "This is our lord Sir Dumbtaro's chariot."

LADIES.   Very well. We will put "Sir" in front of your name.

DUMBTARO.   Now you both lock your arms.

LADIES.   We will.

DUMBTARO.   Let me get up and try.   Good!   March on!

LADIES.   Very well.

DUMBTARO.   Whose chariot is this?   Whose chariot?

LADIES.   This is, indeed, our lord Sir Dumbtaro's chariot!
Sir Dumbtaro's chariot!

DUMBTARO.   That's good, but louder, louder!   Quick, go on,
go on!

Whose chariot is this?

LADIES.   Our lord Sir Dumbtaro's chariot! . . .

BUSU

Characters: THE LORD OF THE HOUSE, TARO *and* JIRO, *his attendants.*

LORD. I am the master of this household. I wish to summon my houseboys and give them some important instructions today. Taro boy, are you there?

TARO. *Ha!*

LORD. Call Jiro boy too.

TARO. Indeed I will. Jiro boy, Master is calling.

JIRO. Very well.

TARO AND JIRO. Here we are.

LORD. It is nothing very special that I want you for. I am going out for a jaunt, so take good care of the house.

TARO AND JIRO. Very well, sir. We will take good care of the house.

LORD. I have something very important to entrust to you. Wait there!

TARO AND JIRO. *Ha!*

LORD. *Yai, yai!* I am going to entrust this to your care. Guard it well!

TARO AND JIRO. What is that, may we ask?

LORD. This is *busu.*

TARO. Oh, if that is *rusu,* a watchman, then I can go with you.

JIRO. I, too, would like to go with you.

LORD. What? What did you think I said?

TARO. I thought you said that was *rusu.* That is the reason I suggested accompanying you.

84

LORD. You are mistaken. I said this is a *busu*, a deadly poison. Be careful, for even if the wind from that direction touches you, you will be killed. Never under any circumstances go near it, but guard it well.

TARO. If it is as dangerous as that, why does my master keep it in the house?

LORD. That is indeed a very reasonable question. I will tell you. The *busu* belongs to the lord of the house, and handled by him, it is not only harmless but also very useful. But should anyone else touch it, he dies instantly. So do not go near it, but guard it well from a distance.

TARO. If that is the case . . .

JIRO. We will be careful.

LORD. I shall not be very long.

TARO AND JIRO. We will be waiting for your return. (*The lord goes out.*)

TARO. That is that! Very good. Now we can visit with each other without any interference.

JIRO. We have never been left by ourselves so nicely as this.

TARO. Wherever master went, he has always taken one of us with him. This is most extraordinary. That *busu* must be exceedingly valuable.

JIRO. As you say, since he has left us to guard it, it must be something very valuable.

TARO. Oh, mercy!

JIRO. What is the matter?

TARO. A gust of wind came from the direction of the *busu*, and I thought that was the last of me.

JIRO. That was not wind.

TARO. Lucky it wasn't. Well, I have a notion to look at that *busu*.

JIRO.   I dare say! You are indeed a reckless fellow. Master told us that he can handle it, but if anyone else touches it, he will be killed instantly. Don't be silly!

TARO.   What you say is true enough. But suppose by chance someone asks us: "I hear your master has a thing called *busu*, but what is it like?" We cannot very well say we have no idea what it is, can we? I will have just a peek.

JIRO.   What you say is reasonable enough, but if the wind kills us, what will happen if we have a peek? Let it alone.

TARO.   That is the point. If the wind from that direction kills us, we must not get in the wind. You fan while I take a look.

JIRO.   Take a look while fanning? That is a good idea.

TARO.   Then I will fan while you untie the cord.

JIRO.   All right. Fan hard, please, while I am about it.

TARO.   All right.

JIRO.   Fan hard, hard!

TARO.   I am. I am fanning.

JIRO.   Coming! Coming!

TARO.   Go on! Go on!

JIRO.   It's untied.

TARO.   Good! Now you take the cover off.

JIRO.   Since I untied the cord, you take the cover off.

TARO.   All right. You fan as hard as you can.

JIRO.   I certainly will.

TARO.   Coming! Fan hard! It is off. Anyway it is not a monster, I see.

JIRO.   How do you know?

TARO.   If it were, it would fly at us. I know now it is not.

JIRO.   Right you are.

TARO.   Now I am going to have a look. Fan hard, hard. Hee-hee, I have seen it.

JIRO.   How does it look?

TARO.   Something whitish.

JIRO.   Let me have a look. I can't see. Oh, I call that a bit grayish.

TARO.   *Yum, yum!* It looks good. I want to taste it.

JIRO.   Don't be a fool! You will die this instant. Let it alone. If the wind kills us, what would happen when you eat it?

TARO.   I am bewitched by that *busu*. I cannot help it even if I am killed! I am going to taste it.

JIRO.   Master entrusted it to us. You can't have it while there is any breath in me.

TARO.   Let go of my sleeve.

JIRO.   I cannot, while I am here.

TARO.   Let go now.

JIRO.   I cannot.

TARO.   Let go, I say.

JIRO.   Never, never.

TARO (*chanting*).   Tearing away from detaining hands, I approach this strange thing, *busu*.

JIRO.   How awful! My companion will be killed this instant.

TARO.   Oh, oh! I cannot resist it. I cannot.

JIRO.   Come, come! What is the matter?

TARO.   *Yum, yum!* My tongue is melting in my mouth! Wonderful!

JIRO.   What is it? What is it?

TARO.   It's sugar!

JIRO.   Let me taste it, too. Sure, it is.

TARO.   Master fooled us. Delicious! I cannot leave it alone. Give it to me.

JIRO.   Don't eat it all up by yourself. Let me have a little of it.

TARO.   You have some too. But, look! You have eaten it all up. That is a pretty thing, indeed. I will tell Master as soon as he comes back.

JIRO.　Now look here. You first opened it even when I told you not to. I will tell him that.

TARO.　That's a joke, but this is terrible. What had we better do?

JIRO.　Indeed, what can we do?

TARO.　I have a scheme. Tear that precious scroll which Master is so fond of.

JIRO.　What a reckless fellow you are! Tear the scroll on top of eating the *busu?* I can't.

TARO.　I have an idea; so go ahead.

JIRO.　*Sara, sara!* There I have done it.

TARO.　Well done. I will tell him when he comes back.

JIRO.　Now look here! You told me to do it, and that is unfair.

TARO.　*Ha, ha!* That was a joke. Now you smash the big bowl and the stand.

JIRO.　You must be out of your mind. They are Master's pet treasures. I can't.

TARO.　Go on! They all help to get us out of the difficulty.

JIRO.　All right, then. *Garan, chin, gara-rin!*

TARO.　Very good! Set up a big howl when you hear Master coming.

JIRO.　Will howling help us?

TARO.　Sure! I hear him coming. Come this way.

LORD.　I have taken a stroll very leisurely. My boys must be waiting for me. I must hasten home.
　　Yai, yai! Taro boy and Jiro boy! I have come home.

TARO.　He is here. Howl hard.

TARO AND JIRO.　*Wa-wo-wa, boo-waa!*

LORD.　What is this all about? Instead of coming out to welcome me, they start weeping bitterly. What is the matter?

TARO.　Jiro boy, you speak up.

JIRO.   No, you tell him, please.

LORD.   One of you, tell me quickly.

TARO.   Then I will tell my master.   After you went out, we became a little lonesome, and Jiro suggested that we wrestle together.   I told him that I had never wrestled before, but as he insisted, we began.   But Jiro was so good that he tripped me up several times.   In order to protect myself, I clutched at that scroll, and as — you — see — it — got — that —

JIRO.   As you see, it got . . .   (*Both weep.*)

LORD.   Good gracious!   The most precious scroll, and you tore it to pieces.   Unpardonable!   What else did you do?

TARO.   And he caught me by the waist and threw me over that bowl and the stand, and they broke . . .

JIRO.   To pieces . . .

LORD.   This is an inexcusable outrage.   What shall I do to you?   Is there anything else?

TARO.   We were so mortified that we decided to kill ourselves at once, and since you told us that the *busu* in the box would kill us instantly, we opened the box and ate it.   But unfortunately we are not dead yet.

JIRO.   Alas, not yet.

TARO.   As death came not with a mouthful, I took another mouthful.   Yet no death.

JIRO.   Three mouthfuls and four mouthfuls!   Alas, I could not die.

TARO.   Even five and six!   Alas, no!

TARO AND JIRO.   Though we have taken ten mouthfuls, nay all that there was of the *busu*, yet are we alive.   Our lives are charmed.   They have not come to their appointed close.

LORD.   You confounded scoundrels!

TARO AND JIRO.   Pardon us!   Pardon us!

LORD.   Never, never!   Running away?   Catch them, catch them!

LITERATE HIGHWAYMEN
(*Fumi Yamadachi*)

Characters: GENDAYU, CHOBEI.

GENDAYU (*As if in fright, he walks backward and shouts.*)   Get him, get him!   Don't you dare to let him go through here!

CHOBEI.   Let's go!   Let's go!
   Hey you there!   Why didn't you get in action?

GENDAYU.   Because you shouted "Let go!   Let go!"   I thought the fellow was either your friend or relative, and let him go unharmed.

CHOBEI.   I said "Let us go!"   Don't you know the password of highwaymen?   It means the fellow is rich and we should rob him.

GENDAYU.   If that was what you meant, why didn't you say so?   Look!   How fast the fellow flees!

CHOBEI.   Who would not?   But alas!   This all comes from your being so cowardly.   My bad luck began when I became your ally.   No more of this.   (*So saying, he throws his spear on the ground.*)

GENDAYU.   If you do not want to be with me, that's all right.   But why did you throw your spear?

CHOBEI.   I did it purposely.   If you do not know what I meant, I will tell you: "Out with you!"

GENDAYU.   Hum!   You dared, did you?   (*He throws his bow and arrow.*)

CHOBEI.   Hey!   Why did you throw your bow and arrow?

GENDAYU.   To trample you under.

CHOBEI.   I am a man.   I am not going to be trampled under
(*They begin to fight.*)

GENDAYU.   Stop! Don't push me so hard.   There is a
bramble bush behind me.

CHOBEI.   What of a bramble bush to one who is to die in a few
minutes?

GENDAYU.   All right.

CHOBEI.   Wait! Wait for a moment.

GENDAYU.   What?

CHOBEI.   Don't push me so.   I shall fall off a precipice.

GENDAYU.   What of a precipice to you who is to be killed?

CHOBEI.   Say!

GENDAYU.   What?

CHOBEI.   The way we are grappling with each other must be a
wonderful sight.

GENDAYU.   Ah indeed.   I should like to show it to all the
manly men.

CHOBEI.   If we should die now, no one will see this heroic
scene.   Moreover, who is going to notify our wives and
children of our tragic end.   Our dying is utterly wasted, I fear.

GENDAYU.   What you say is very true.   No one will let our
families know about it.

CHOBEI.   We might leave a note of farewell.   What do you
think?

GENDAYU.   That is an excellent idea.
    But our arms are locked tightly.   There is no way of unlock-
ing them.

CHOBEI.   That's simple.   Let's say "One, two, three," and at
"three" we will both unlock them.

GENDAYU.   Very well.

BOTH.   One! Two!

CHOBEI.   The last one, and I am not going to be beaten.

GENDAYU.   Look here! We no longer are fighting. Let us withdraw our arms peacefully.

CHOBEI.   Very well.
By the by, have you a brush and ink?

GENDAYU.   No, I have not.

CHOBEI.   I have. I brought them in case we get many valuables and have to make out a list.

GENDAYU.   You are a clever fellow.

CHOBEI.   You compose a note and I will write it.

GENDAYU.   Very well.   But what shall we say?

CHOBEI.   Indeed, what shall we say?

GENDAYU.   "At this auspicious occasion of the New Year —." How about that?

CHOBEI.   When we are about to die, we can hardly call the occasion auspicious.

GENDAYU.   What you say is true enough, but how shall we begin?

CHOBEI.   I wonder.

GENDAYU.   How about "I beg your pardon to write a few lines?"

CHOBEI.   No, no! The occasion is much too acute for that sort of rhetoric.
Never mind.   I will compose a fitting message.

GENDAYU.   Please do so.
Oh, how he writes!   The tip of his brush is actually dancing.

CHOBEI.   Here!   I have finished it.

GENDAYU.   What did you say?

CHOBEI.   I started out, "To get back to the very beginning —."

GENDAYU.   That's good.

CHOBEI (*reading*).   "To get back to the very beginning, by a strange mishap I ran away from my family and became a highwayman who robbed innocent travellers and priests.   But alas, I had quarrelled with my fellow highwayman, and after a long and hard grappling, I grabbed my sword . . .''

GENDAYU (*jumping up*).   Oh, you betrayer!

CHOBEI.   What is the matter?

GENDAYU.   You said, "Grab hold of my sword," and I thought you were going to attack me.

CHOBEI.   That was only a sentence.

GENDAYU.   Oh, only a sentence!   Why didn't you tell me? I nearly fainted with fright.

CHOBEI.   I am sorry.   Then let us read this together.

BOTH.   "I grabbed my sword.   But wait!   Should I die here without witness, people may think I was killed by unworthy fellows.   But, my dear wife, I want you to remember my story, and honor and narrate correctly my tragic fate.

"Alas, when I think of my wife and children whom I leave behind, I cannot keep back my tears. . . .''   (*They both cry.*)

CHOBEI.   What a tragic affair this is!

GENDAYU.   It is.

CHOBEI.   How about postponing our dying for a little while?

GENDAYU.   Since no one has heard our resolution to die, our honor is not violated in postponing it.   We may do so.

CHOBEI.   Then how long shall we postpone it?

GENDAYU.   Five days?

CHOBEI.   That seems too short.   A little longer perhaps?

GENDAYU.   How about a year or two?

CHOBEI.   A year or two pass away in a dream.   Really, come to think of it, no one has seen our altercation, and if we two agree, we can give up this idea entirely.   How about it?

GENDAYU.   What you say is very true.   Let's be friends again.

CHOBEI.   This certainly is felicitous.   Let us chant the adventure of the day and return home together.

GENDAYU.   Excellent.

CHOBEI.   Realizing that to die is utter waste . . .

BOTH.   Hand in hand the two highwaymen
Wend their way to their home.

CHOBEI.   Listen, my friend!

GENDAYU.   What is it?

CHOBEI.   You and I shall live five hundred eighty years.

GENDAYU.   Ah, indeed!   To the end of seven incarnations . . .

BOTH.   Oh, happy day!   Happy day!

THE DEVA KING
(*Niwô*)

Characters: SHITE, WAKI, SPECTATORS.

SHITE.   I dwell in this vicinity, but recently I have met reverses of fortune, and it has become exceedingly difficult for me to live here.   Therefore I will go to a distant country to try my luck anew.   However, as I have a friend who has been very kind to me, I will first call to bid him farewell.   Also he may have a good scheme that will enable me to stay here.   I must hurry.   I hope he is at home.   As he is a very busy person, even though I have come thus far especially, I may be unable to see him.   Here is his establishment.

     Pardon, pardon!   Is anyone home?

WAKI.   Someone is at the gate.   Who is it?

SHITE.   It is I.

WAKI.   Oh, is it you?   I am glad to see you.

SHITE.   I have not seen you for a long while.   I hope you have been well.

WAKI.   Thank you.   We have all been well.   But you look as if you are ready to take a long journey.   Where are you going?

SHITE.   I came to call on you today to talk about that.   I must confess that recently I have met reverses of fortune so that I cannot stay in this city any longer, and I have decided to go to a distant country.   Therefore I have come to bid you farewell.   You have been good to me and I am very grateful to you.

WAKI. I am exceedingly sorry to hear that. Instead of going to a far-off country, isn't there any way of trying out your fortune in this city?

SHITE. I fear not. All possible avenues are closed to me. I cannot very well stay here any longer.

WAKI. But have you someone in a distant country upon whom you can depend?

SHITE. Unfortunately no one, but in desperation I just hit upon that idea.

WAKI. You are a reckless man. What will you do in a strange country with no friends?

SHITE. Precisely.

WAKI. I can't let you do that. I certainly should like to help you out.

SHITE. Please assist me.

WAKI. I have a good idea. Are you a good mimic?

SHITE. That depends on what I am to mimic.

WAKI. Niwô, the Deva King, I am thinking.

SHITE. You mean Niwô whose statue stands in the temple gate?

WAKI. Precisely.

SHITE. Fortunately I have lived in the neighborhood of the temple, and as I remember the statue well, that will be easy.

WAKI. That's splendid! I shall dress you up as an image of Niwô and then send word round that a wonderful image of Niwô has descended in Uyeno Park. I am sure people will come to pay homage.

SHITE. I am certain of that.

WAKI. With what offering you get, you can start out afresh. What do you think of this idea?

SHITE. Excellent indeed, and I am greatly obliged to you. Please go ahead with your scheme.

WAKI.   Then come this way.   I shall dress you up as an image of Niwô.

SHITE.   Very well.

WAKI.   First put this hood on.

SHITE.   Very well.

WAKI.   Slip this over your shoulders.

SHITE.   Does this look all right?

WAKI.   It's almost done.   Let us go to Uyeno Park!   Come.

SHITE.   Very good!   I am a thousand times obliged to you for your kindness.

WAKI.   Needless to say you must be careful not to be detected.

SHITE.   Rest assured on that point.   I will do my utmost to safeguard against that.

WAKI.   Oh, before we know it, we are already in Uyeno Park. Where do you think will be the best place?

SHITE.   Where indeed do you think is the best place?

WAKI.   This looks good.   Come here and mimic a Niwô.

SHITE.   Very well.

WAKI.   Excellent!   You are the very image of Niwô.   I will go and tell people so that they may come and pay homage.

SHITE.   Very good.

WAKI.   Listen, folks!   Just now here in this park, has descended a new and wonderful Niwô.   So come and worship him.

FIRST SPECTATOR.   Are you all there?

CROWD.   Here we are.

FIRST SPECTATOR.   Did you hear that just now a new and wonderful Niwô descended into this park?

CROWD.   So we hear.

FIRST SPECTATOR.   Then let us go and pay homage to him.

CROWD.   Very good.

FIRST SPECTATOR.   Then come.

CROWD.   We shall follow you.

FIRST SPECTATOR.   The descent of a Niwô in this day and age is indeed a miracle.

SECOND SPECTATOR.   As you say, it is really a miracle.

SHITE.   People ought to come very soon.   Well, that crowd looks as if they come to worship.   I'll get myself ready.

FIRST SPECTATOR.   Here we are already in the park.   Where is the image?

SECOND SPECTATOR.   Indeed, where is this Niwô?

FIRST SPECTATOR.   Oh, there he stands.

SECOND SPECTATOR.   Without mistake, there he stands.

FIRST SPECTATOR.   Let us pay homage.   But first let us give an offering.

CROWD.   Certainly.   Very well.

FIRST SPECTATOR.   First let us offer some coins.

CROWD.   Very well.

FIRST SPECTATOR.   Please protect me from all diseases and calamities.

SECOND SPECTATOR.   Please grant me health and wealth.

THIRD SPECTATOR.   Grant peace, happiness, and long life to my family.

FIRST SPECTATOR.   Give me strength, and I will offer this precious sword to you.

SECOND SPECTATOR.   I will present this.

FIRST SPECTATOR.   This is a miraculous Niwô.

CROWD.   This certainly is wondrously miraculous.

FIRST SPECTATOR.   Well, we must be getting home.

SECOND SPECTATOR.   I will tell this wonder far and wide, and urge people to come and worship him.

CROWD.   We will all do so.

FIRST SPECTATOR.   Come, folks.

CROWD.   Coming!

SHITE.   *Ha, ha!* How wonderful! I am very happy. What an abundance of treasure! I must carry the gifts home and examine them.

Hello, hello! Where is my friend?

WAKI.   I am here. What is the matter? Were there any devotees?

SHITE.   Oh, indeed. There was an enormous crowd, and not only did they offer coins, but also these treasures.

WAKI.   Well, well! This is very fortunate. Now you have a little capital to start afresh.

SHITE.   Quite true. Now I have some capital. First I wish to ask you to keep the valuables for me.

WAKI.   All right. I will keep them for you.

SHITE.   Thank you. But, if you please, I'd like to try this game again.

WAKI.   Oh, no! You have enough now.

SHITE.   I shall be careful not to be detected. Please let me try again.

WAKI.   No, that's too dangerous.

SHITE.   Oh, please let me try this once.

WAKI.   Well, if you must, I suppose you must.

SHITE.   Thank you very much.

WAKI.   I will let you carry a sceptre this time.

SHITE.   I am greatly obliged to you.

WAKI.   Do not get caught.

SHITE.   Rest assured. I shall take care of that.

WAKI.   Let us hurry.

SHITE.   Very good. My good luck is all due to your kindness, and I shall be eternally grateful to you. Here we are in Uyeno

Park again. This time I shall try a Niwô with his mouth closed. Is there no one to worship me? Oh, I see people coming!

FIRST MAN. Is everybody here?

CROWD. Here we are!

FIRST MAN. I am told that a new Niwô appeared in Uyeno Park, and I wish to pay homage to him. What do you think?

SECOND MAN. That is excellent. I shall accompany you.

FIRST MAN. Then let us go. Come, one and all.

CROWD. We are following.

FIRST MAN. The descent of a Niwô is wonderfully miraculous!

SECOND MAN. As you say, it is a miracle.

FIRST MAN. We are already in the park.

SECOND MAN. So we are.

FIRST MAN. Where, I wonder, has the noble image descended?

CROWD. Where, indeed?

FIRST MAN. Here he is!

SECOND MAN. Indeed here he stands.

FIRST MAN. Let us first offer some coins.

CROWD. Very well.

FIRST MAN. Now let us worship him.

CROWD. Very well.

FIRST MAN. Grant me fortune and all good virtues.

SECOND MAN. Make my sons and daughters and their sons and daughters prosperous.

FIRST MAN. This indeed is a noble image.

SECOND MAN. Noble he is!

FIRST MAN. Like a living Buddha!

SECOND MAN. Quite so.

FIRST MAN. Quick! Come this way.

SECOND MAN.   What is the matter?

FIRST MAN.   What do you think? If you look into his eyes closely, you will see that his noble eyeballs are moving. Have you noticed that?

SECOND MAN.   As you say! I see his head is moving, too.

FIRST MAN.   This is very strange. I can't understand it. There are many false and wicked monks and priests who take unfair advantage of the public. To find whether this is the real image of Niwô or not, shall I tickle him? What do you think?

SECOND MAN.   Excellent idea, indeed.

FIRST MAN.   Then come closer.

SECOND MAN.   Very well.

FIRST MAN.   This is a wonderfully wrought image.

SECOND MAN.   Truly it is.

FIRST MAN.   His head seems to be moving.

SECOND MAN.   Morever, his eyeballs are rolling in their sockets.

FIRST MAN.   Just like a living man's.

SECOND MAN.   Just so.

FIRST MAN.   Tickle, tickle!

SECOND MAN.   Tickle, tickle!

SHITE.   Ouch, *ha, ha!* Ouch, *ha, ha!* Forgive me, forgive me!

FIRST MAN.   You naughty monk! You wicked imposter!

SHITE.   Pardon, pardon! Oh, please spare my life.

CROWD.   You cheat! You scoundrel! Is there no one here to catch him? Do not let him get away! Catch him, catch him!

AN UNFAIR EXCHANGE
(*Sarugai Kôtô*)

Characters: A BLIND MAN, HIS WIFE, A MONKEY MAN.

BLIND MAN. I am a blind man who dwells in the capital. I hear the cherry blossoms are at their height now. Every year my wife teases me to take her to see them, but since I cannot see anything, I am loath to go, and every year she loses her temper. This year, however, I will take her to Kiyomizu, and though I cannot see them with eyes, I will try to smell them. Hello, my wife! Are you there?

WIFE. What is it that you call for me?

BLIND MAN. Oh, it is nothing very special that I called you for. I hear the blossoms are at their best now. Because you have been wishing to go every year, I have decided to take you to see the flowers. You look and enjoy while I smell them.

WIFE. I am very happy to hear this. It will be a pleasant diversion. But flowers are for the eye, and I have never heard of smelling them.

BLIND MAN. No, no. It is all right to smell them. Listen, there is an old poem on the matter.

> In moonlight night
> > The white blossom is out of sight;
> > Yet by her fragrance, I can tell
> > Where she does dwell.

So you see, it is perfectly all right to smell flowers.

WIFE. Indeed I am convinced. Let us go then!

BLIND MAN. Lead me by the hand, please.

WIFE. Very well.

BLIND MAN.   Listen! To go with you hand in hand thus is perfect bliss. To me it is better than looking at cherry blossoms.

WIFE.   Oh, please do not be so loving. People might hear us.

BLIND MAN.   What a crowd! I suppose they are all going to see the cherries.

WIFE.   I believe so.

BLIND MAN.   Did you prepare a little flask for us?

WIFE.   Yes, I sent it to the temple at Kiyomizu. It will be waiting for us there.

BLIND MAN.   That's excellent.

WIFE.   Oh, please! Strolling along, we have already come to the temple ground of Kiyomizu.

BLIND MAN.   Already? Let us pick out a secluded place.

WIFE.   Here is a nice place. Come this way and sit down. The flowers are indeed marvelous.

BLIND MAN.   I shall sit down. You sit here too. Well, first let us have a little *sake*. Take the bottle out.

WIFE.   Very well. Here is a cup.

BLIND MAN.   All right. Please pour me some.

WIFE.   Here!

BLIND MAN.   This is delicious. Somehow it does taste better out-of-doors than at home. You have one too.

WIFE.   Thanks. I will.

BLIND MAN.   Take a full cup. How about a little song?

BOTH.   *Zan-za!* The waves of Hamamatsu roar. *Za-zan-za!*

WIFE.   Have another cup!

BLIND MAN.   Good! The more I drink, the better it gets. Let us sing some more.

MONKEY MAN.   I am a monkey man who has been making the rounds of the capital recently. Today I have been visiting my patrons, but I hear the cherry blossoms are at their height.

As the temple of Kiyomizu is on my way home, I think I shall stop there.

Oh, already I am at Kiyomizu. What a crowd, indeed! *Ha*, there is a blind man looking at the flowers with his wife. What an uncommonly beautiful woman she is! (*He goes toward her stealthily, and speaks to her in a low voice.*)

Oh, hello, my dear lady! I want to ask you something.

WIFE.   What is the matter, I wonder. Were you speaking to me?

MONKEY MAN.   Yes, indeed. I was talking to you. Is that your husband?

WIFE.   Yes, and we have known each other ever since we were so high.

MONKEY MAN.   It is a great pity that such a singularly pretty girl like you is married to a blind man. I will arrange an infinitely better match for you. So you come with me.

WIFE.   That is very good of you. Though I am tempted, I have known my husband so long that I feel sorry to leave him.

BLIND MAN.   Hey, my wife! Where have you gone?

WIFE.   I am right here.

BLIND MAN.   I cannot understand this at all. Where have you been?

WIFE.   I just went over there to get a little more *sake*.

BLIND MAN.   I still can't understand this. Give me some more. Pour it for me, quick!

WIFE.   There you are. Have as much as you like!

BLIND MAN.   *Ha!* This is good. Now you have one. I will pour for you.

WIFE.   I fear I shall get light-hearted. But then, what does it matter! I'll have a cup. As there is no one around, how about a little dance to relish the *sake?*

BLIND MAN.   Just as you say. To get a little light-hearted and to dance! That's excellent.

WIFE. I am so happy! Do dance, please. (*The blind man dances while his wife chants.*)

> In this blessed land of Yamato,
>> Peace reigns o'er land and sea.
> May thy reign, my sovereign lord,
>> Last ages, myriad ages . . .

MONKEY MAN. What do I see? The blind man is dancing. (*He motions to the wife.*)

Listen, dear lady! Please come here a moment.

WIFE. What is it?

MONKEY MAN. I will arrange the best possible marriage for you. So you get out of this right away and come with me.

WIFE. I am not uninterested in your proposal, but will it be a very good house?

MONKEY MAN. Oh, sure! It is an excellent family. Furthermore the man is very handsome.

WIFE. If that is the case, I think I can manage to come with you.

BLIND MAN. Oh, oh, my dear wife! Where have you gone? Wife, my wife!

WIFE. I am right here.

That was a splendid performance of dancing you gave. A very pretty show!

BLIND MAN. You are getting up and down and up and down all the time. I cannot understand why all this fuss. I have an idea.

I will tie her with this sash and fasten her to my belt.

WIFE. What under the sun are you doing?

BLIND MAN. Now I have no need to be anxious about her. Come, come! I want to drink more *sake*.

WIFE. There, I have poured it for you. I am afraid you are going beyond your limit.

MONKEY MAN. What is this? Sure enough, the blind man is clever. He has tied his wife to his belt.

Now come, please! Oh, I see! She means she is tied and cannot come. Of course! But I have a scheme. I will tie my monkey to that sash instead. I must be very quiet so that he will not hear me. *Ha*, that's done. (*After tying the monkey to the sash, he goes off with the wife to a corner of the stage.*)

Listen! I told you that I would arrange a marriage for you, but that is a lie; I want you to marry me. We will live together one thousand, nay, nay, ten thousand years happily. Get on my back, and I will carry you home. Oh, how happy I am! Let us hurry home! (*They go off.*)

BLIND MAN. *Ha*, my wife! I want to drink more *sake*. Pour it for me. But why don't you say something? Well, well, she is angry because I tied her. Does that make you so mad? Come, come! Be good. (*He pulls the sash.*)

MONKEY. *Kya, kya, kya!*

BLIND MAN. Now, now, wife! Why do you scratch me so? What is the matter?

MONKEY. *Kya, kya, kya!*

BLIND MAN. Oh, how sad! My wife has turned into a monkey and is hairy all over. Alas, alack! What can I do?

MONKEY. *Kya, kya, kya!*

BLIND MAN. Alas, alack! Do not scratch me so! Do forgive me, my dear wife!

SEED OF HŌJŌ
(Hōjō no Tane)

Characters: A NEPHEW, AN UNCLE.

NEPHEW.   I am an inhabitant of this vicinity. I have an uncle over across the mountain whom I often call on. He is such a clever story-teller that I am always taken in, and it is very provoking. But today I intend to make up a few good stories myself to dupe him.

Indeed, my uncle is a clever person. He tells so many stories that once in a while I should think he would repeat himself, but not so. I have never heard him tell a story which even resembles others. Tonight I have made up tall ones, and I am sure he cannot beat me this time.

As I amble along, here I am already. I must inquire. Pardon me! Are you in?

UNCLE.   Well, well! I have not seen you for a long while. What has been the trouble?

NEPHEW.   Oh, I made a pilgrimage to Mt. Fuji recently, and that is why I had not called on you before.

UNCLE.   That was very commendable of you. Was the journey up exciting?

NEPHEW.   Indeed, it was very jolly.

By the by, Fuji is much larger and higher than I imagined.

UNCLE.   It should be, for it's the most famous mountain in the world. Was there anything interesting?

NEPHEW.   No, nothing special, but after we entered the province of Kai, we stayed over night at the foot of the mountain. There was a crowd of pilgrims, and in the course of conversa-

107

tion, we younger men thought it would be fun to put a paper bag over Fuji. The older folks thought it impossible and laughed at us. Then we said we could.

Immediately the fellows brought out bamboo spoons, and each holding one in his mouth, two in his hands, and two more in his feet, we began to make paste. In no time we made it as high as the mountain. Next we collected all the paper from the provinces of Idzu and Suruga. First I thought we were to make a huge bag, but the fellows began to paste paper on the mountain, and in no time we were at the top of Fuji, which was all clothed with a paper bag. Wasn't that an unheard-of thing?

UNCLE.   Oh, no! That is not so unusual.

Last year when I went down to Omi Province, the young men brewed tea in Lake Biwa and drank up the whole lake.

NEPHEW.   There you are up to your old tricks. How could they possibly drink the lake dry?

UNCLE.   Listen. They said, "Let's make tea in the lake," and gathered up all the tea leaves, irrespective of their quality, from the five neighboring provinces. In no time there was a pile of tea leaves as high as Mikami Hill. Then they put it in the lake, and young fellows with mulberry brooms with handles one hundred feet long began to stir it. When it was done, they blew off froth and drank it up. In fact they drank the whole lake dry, but the froth they blew off still remains and is known as Awazu ga Hara, Plain of Froth.

NEPHEW.   Oh, but you are telling an old yarn again. The Plain of Awazu appears in the heroic tale of Kiso Yoshinaka.

UNCLE.   But you don't know the New Plain of Awazu right beside it, which appeared last year.

NEPHEW.   That's a lie.

UNCLE.   If you think it a lie, you just go and look for it yourself.

NEPHEW.   I shall not argue with you.

But please listen! A few years ago, when I went to the western part of the country, I saw a bull that lay down in Innami Plain of Harima Province, and fed on the pastures of Awaji Island. Imagine feeding himself across those mountains, rivers, and sea. Don't you think it was an enormous beast?

UNCLE. That's not so wonderful. When I went to Kwanto last time, I saw a drum nine miles in circumference.

NEPHEW. How ridiculous! You can make the frame of a drum by joining pieces of wood, but I fear you cannot find a hide nine miles large.

UNCLE. Oh, but how do you know there is not? To tell you the truth, I verified the fact that it was made of the bull hide which you saw on Innami Plain.

NEPHEW. Great Scott! I am taken in again.

I confess, because you always fool me so successfully, that I decided to trick you once and made up these stories, but you are too clever for me.

Tell me how you manage to collect such marvelous stories.

UNCLE. At your pace, you will never be able to beat me. Though I shall never tell any outsiders, you are an exception. I will tell you the secret.

NEPHEW. What is it?

UNCLE. There is a seed for such stories known as the *Hôjô no Tane*. Would you like to have one?

NEPHEW. Oh, please give me one.

UNCLE. Just wait there a few minutes.

NEPHEW. Very well.

UNCLE (*aside*). What do you think of this? There are some fools in this world. He wants to have a seed of lies, and I am going to have some fun with him.

Here, my dear nephew! I will give you a seed.

NEPHEW. Please!

UNCLE. I buried it in the garden. Dig it up.

NEPHEW. Very well.

UNCLE. I think it was by that stepping stone.

NEPHEW. Here?

UNCLE. Yes, dig there.

NEPHEW. No, it is not here.

UNCLE. Dig a little deeper.

NEPHEW. I cannot find it.

UNCLE. Now I remember. It was under this pine tree.

NEPHEW. Very well.

UNCLE. There, right there.

NEPHEW. I cannot find it.

UNCLE. Dig deeper.

NEPHEW. Yes, I dug deep, but it was not there.

UNCLE. You are indeed a silly fellow. That which you cannot find is called the *Hōjō no Tane*.

NEPHEW. Was that a lie too?

UNCLE. Of course! What did you think it was? *Ha, ha, ha!*

NEPHEW. Even if you are my uncle, this is too much. I cannot let you get away. Catch him! catch him!

PLOP! CLICK!
(*Dobu Kacchiri*)

Characters: THE KÔTÔ, KIKUICHI, A PASSER-BY.

KÔTÔ. ´ I am a Kôtô [1] who dwells in this vicinity. Now I will call Kikuichi and consult with him. Is Kikuichi around?

KIKUICHI. Coming!

KÔTÔ. Where are you?

KIKUICHI. Right here.

KÔTÔ. It is nothing very special that I want you for. As I have not been out for a long while, time seems to hang heavily on my hands. I wish to take a short sight-seeing trip. What do you think about it?

KIKUICHI. To tell you the truth, I was just going to suggest it to you. It is an excellent idea.

KÔTÔ. Then let us go. Get ready a *sake* flask.

KIKUICHI. Very well. The *sake* flask is ready.

KÔTÔ. Let us go at once. Come!

KIKUICHI. I am ready.

KÔTÔ. What do you think? It must strike some people as ridiculous to see blind men like us go on a sight-seeing trip. But going to a new place changes one's mood and is pleasant.

KIKUICHI. No one, I am sure, will think us ridiculous. Therefore, whenever you are so moved, we must have as many such jaunts as possible. They do you much good, Master.

[1] By an edict of 1547, two official ranks were created for educated blind-men, such as musicians and scholars, the first being Kengyô and the second Kôtô.

111

KÔTÔ.   Already we are out of town.   We must be out in the open fields.   It is rather lonesome here.

KIKUICHI.   This is indeed an open field.

KÔTÔ.   When I am in the open plain my heart expands, and I feel light-hearted.

KIKUICHI.   As you say, it is very delightful.

KÔTÔ.   Listen!   I have long been intending to tell you that you cannot forever be singing little ditties and reciting light tales.   How about practicing the *Battle of the Heike*,[1] the famous epic?

KIKUICHI.   I have been hoping to ask your help in that matter. Fortunately now you have brought the subject up yourself. If you can teach me that, I shall be exceedingly grateful to you.

KÔTÔ.   Then I will.   Since there seems to be no one around, I will recite a verse for you.

KIKUICHI.   That is very kind of you.   I shall listen

KÔTÔ.   "Now the battle of Ichi no Tani had come to a crisis, and there was a great combat.   The noble Heike, alas, were defeated, and the warriors of the Genji, eager to win fame, crashed forward in their attack.   The Heike fell like wheat before the scythe.   What bloodshed! What confusion!   Some had their chins cut off; some their heels.   Confused amidst the din of cries and groans, they clapped the severed heels on their bleeding chins and the severed chins on their bleeding heels.   Ah, the strange sight indeed!   Three or four hundred battle-scarred soldiers with beards on their heels and blisters on their chins! . . ."

KIKUICHI.   That is indeed very marvelous.   I am happy to have heard it.

KÔTÔ.   Let us go a little further.   Come, follow me!

KIKUICHI.   I am following.

[1] Fought in the province of Settsu in the year 1185.

KÔTÔ.   There are many who chant the *Heike*, but none I know can do it well.   So you must practice hard.

KIKUICHI.   I will practice very hard, and I hope you will again instruct me.

KÔTÔ.   If I should be appointed to the position of a "Kengyô," I shall try to make you a "Kôtô."

KIKUICHI.   That is very good of you, to be sure.

KÔTÔ.   What?   I hear the ripple of water.   We must be near a river.

KIKUICHI.   True, it seems like a river.

KÔTÔ.   We must cross over.   What had we better do?

KIKUICHI.   Indeed what should we do?

PASSER-BY (*aside*).   I dwell nearby here.   As I have a little business across the mountains, I must hasten.   What!   Two blind men are going to cross the river.   I wonder how they are going to do it.   I will stop and watch them a while.

KÔTÔ.   Come!   Throw a stone and try the depth of the river.

KIKUICHI.   Very well.   *Eh*, there it goes.   *Plop!*

KÔTÔ.   Very deep there.

KIKUICHI.   It is exceedingly deep there.

KÔTÔ.   Try another direction.

KIKUICHI.   Very well.   *Eh*, there it goes.   *Click!*

KÔTÔ.   Shallow there.

KIKUICHI.   Indeed, it seems shallow there.

KÔTÔ.   Then let us wade through.   Come!

KIKUICHI.   But, master, will you wait just a moment?

KÔTÔ.   What is the matter?

KIKUICHI.   I will carry you on my back.

KÔTÔ.   Oh, no.   That is not necessary.   You follow me.

KIKUICHI.   But I am here with you to do just such service. It is for the good of my soul.   Please let me carry you.

KÔTÔ.   No, no. Since you too cannot see, there might be an accident. We will hold on to each other and wade. Come!

KIKUICHI.   But this is my only chance to be of real service to you. I must carry you on my back.

KÔTÔ.   Since you insist, I shall let you carry me. But first we must get ready. Prepare yourself then.

KIKUICHI.   Very well.

PASSER-BY (*aside*).   How clever the blind men are! They try the depth of water with pebbles. I am a lucky dog. I am going to be carried across. (*He climbs on* KIKUICHI's *back.*)

KIKUICHI.   Please hang on to me tightly. Now I am going to wade into the water. I hope it is not going to be very deep.
    Very good indeed. I have done it with perfect ease, and I am glad we had no accident.

PASSER-BY (*aside*).   This was really an unexpected fortune. I am very happy.

KÔTÔ.   Hello, Kikuichi! How about it? Are you ready? No answer? I cannot understand this. Ki-ku-i-chi! Where-are-you?

KIKUICHI.   Y-e-s!

KÔTÔ.   Why don't you carry me across quickly?

KIKUICHI.   But I have just carried you across.

KÔTÔ.   Carried me across? I was just getting ready. You have not carried me across yet. The miserable wretch has gone over all by himself.

KIKUICHI (*hurrying back to the other side*).   When did you cross over on this side again, Master?

KÔTÔ.   When, indeed! The wretch! He is backing out. Come quickly and take me over.

KIKUICHI.   I cannot understand this at all. Well, I will cross over again. Now please climb up on my back.

KÔTÔ.   Be steady.

KIKUICHI.   I am going to wade. This seems very deep.

KÔTÔ.   Be careful and steady.

KIKUICHI.   Yes, yes. But how deep this is! Oh, help, help!

PASSER-BY.   This is highly entertaining. Poor wretches!

KÔTÔ.   Well, well, this is annoying. I am soaked to my bare skin. That was why I refused to be carried across.

KIKUICHI.   I am very sorry. I will wring you out. Though I was going very cautiously, I stumbled. Please forgive me.

KÔTÔ.   It was pure accident, and no one can help that. Did anything happen to the *sake* flask?

KIKUICHI.   What did you say? Oh, the flask is here, quite safe.

KÔTÔ.   I am getting chilly. Pour me out a drink.

KIKUICHI.   Very well.

PASSER-BY.   Another piece of good luck. I shall get a drink.

KIKUICHI.   I am pouring. *Glug, glug!*

KÔTÔ.   Oh, that's enough. I shall forget the chill when I take this.

KIKUICHI.   Of that I am quite certain.

PASSER-BY (*aside*).   How delicious this is!

KÔTÔ.   Kikuichi, my boy! Why didn't you give me some?

KIKUICHI.   But I did pour you some just now.

KÔTÔ.   I thought you did, but there is not a drop in my cup.

KIKUICHI.   I simply cannot understand this. I will pour you some again. Have a cup brimful.

KÔTÔ.   All right. Be quick.

KIKUICHI.   Very well. *Glug, glug!*

PASSER-BY (*aside*).   Another treat! Marvelous *sake* indeed!

KÔTÔ.   That is enough. You take some, too.

KIKUICHI.   May I? That is very kind of you. Wonderful *sake!*

turn. Though conventionalized, the mere sight of him vivifies the comic spell.

The comic nature of the plot in the *kyôgen* is most frequently physical; it is a matter of situation rather than character. Hence incongruity and mistakes produce an emotional shock, and the audience laughs. In the *Ribs and the Cover*, the priest's instruction to his stupid novice comes just one step behind the actual situation. Therefore, when the man comes to borrow a horse, the novice delivers the speech which he was supposed to use when someone comes to borrow an umbrella. He delivers the speech on a horse to a man who later comes to invite the priest to a dinner. This is an age-old method used to produce laughter.[38]

The Japanese from early times made good use of repetition and exaggeration. In the year 484 when Chief Wodate became governor of Harima Province, there was a great feast. In the course of the evening when two children were made to dance, one of them said:

"Do thou the elder brother dance first."

The elder brother said:

"Do thou the younger brother dance first."

They kept this up several times and the company laughed heartily.[39] This type of excessive courtesy often was used in the *kyôgen*. When the country gentleman in the *Gargoyle* stops lamenting over his homely wife, he decides to laugh, and turning to his attendant, says:

"Come, you laugh first."

Innate politeness forbids Taro from doing such a thing.

"No, sir! Please, you first."

They repeat this several times before they finally burst out laughing, but long before they do, the audience is in hearty laughter.

[38] The same method is used in "Der gescheidte Hans" in the *Kinder und Hausmarchen* by the Brothers Grimm.

[39] Chamberlain's *Translation of "Kojiki,"* p. 397.

Popular superstitions played an important part in the *kyôgen*. I have already mentioned the rôle of devils or Japanese *oni* in the folk-lore. The *Tangerine Dealer* and the *Aunt's Sake* are based on the fright of the *oni*. The descent of the Niwô in the *Deva King* is based on popular belief in the efficacy of this deity.

Unlike the Western comedy, there is little trace of love interest in the *kyôgen*, for a Japanese takes the relation of man and woman as a matter of fact and attaches to it no romance. His marriage is arranged, and his wife is a necessary unit in that social institution called family. This sentiment is well expressed in the words of the country gentleman of the *Gargoyle* :

> "I was a fool to get so wrought up over my homely wife in the country. Though I cannot care for her, she has given me many marvelous sons who are my wealth and future hope. That is wondrously lucky for me."

It has often been asked how the feudal regime tolerated the *kyôgen* to be played at their official functions, for more than half of the extant plays deal with the members of the feudal clan in a not too favorable light. The braggart, the coward, the fop, and the hypocrite all appear as feudal lords. Some scholars claim that the so-called feudal lords in the *kyôgen* are the poverty-stricken and degenerated courtiers of Kyoto in disguise; hence the feudal dignitaries took a great delight in the plays. The explanation, however, is slightly strained when one considers how a *kyôgen* master in 1424 was severely punished because he staged a play depicting the destitute condition of the nobles in the imperial court.[40]

Feudal lords of the *kyôgen* to me are feudal lords, and none other. Here we touch upon the perplexing problem of aesthetics. Professor Parker says:

> "The comical object, the thing that makes us laugh or smile and gives us the pleasure of laughter and smiling, is the thing which emphatically contrasts with what is

[40] *Kambun Nikki* [Things Seen and Heard] under the 11th day, 3rd month, 1424.

THE AUNT'S SAKE
(*Oba ga Sake*)

Characters: AN AUNT, A NEPHEW.

AUNT.   I am a woman who dwells at the foot of a hill.   As this is an exceedingly beautiful day, I wish to set up a *sake* shop. Here is a fine place.   I will set it up here.   It looks good.

Listen, folks!   I have set up a shop, so if you wish to have good *sake*, please call on me.

NEPHEW.   I am a youth who dwells in this vicinity.   I have an aunt at the foot of the hill, and as I was told that she has set up a *sake* shop this day, I come to congratulate her, and also be treated by her.   Well, I must hurry.   But by nature my aunt is a miser, so even if I come as far as this, she may not treat me.   That, however, may depend on my tact.

Oh, this must be my aunt's shop.

Pardon, pardon!   Is anyone around?

AUNT.   I am in.

NEPHEW.   How do you do?   I have not seen you for a long while.   I hope you are well.

AUNT.   Very well, thank you.   But what has brought you here today?

NEPHEW.   It is nothing very special, but as the day is fine and I heard you had set up a *sake* shop, I came to congratulate you.

AUNT.   Yes as you say the day is excellent, and I am happy to set up a shop.

NEPHEW.   Though this place seems a little out of the way, there is a fair amount of traffic, and I am quite sure you will be a success.

AUNT.   You are right. Since you come in contact with young fellows, you must tell them the wonder of your aunt's *sake*. That is the way to make this shop a success.

NEPHEW.   Indeed, rest assured. That I will do. I will broadcast far and wide the merits of your *sake*. But first treat me with a drink.

AUNT.   Naturally I would very much like to treat you, but I have not had the so-called lucky opening sale and cannot treat you today. Come again; then I will.

NEPHEW.   Do not stand on ceremony with me, dear aunt. I am not a stranger; I am just one of the family. Treat me to just a cup, please.

AUNT.   No, I can't treat you today. Come again and I promise you a drink.

NEPHEW.   But look here! I am not begging it simply because I want a drink. You see if I am to tell my friends about your *sake*, they will naturally ask me if it is good. I cannot very well say that I do not know, can I? Give me just one drink as a sample.

AUNT.   What a headstrong fellow you are! Under no circumstances can I treat you today. I told you, come again.

NEPHEW.   Are you sure you can't treat me?

AUNT.   I am dead certain of that.

NEPHEW.   Then I must be going. Farewell!

AUNT.   Farewell.
    Gone, at last!

NEPHEW.   What a stingy aunt I have! To come this distance purposely to get a drink and have to return without even a drop is hard luck. What had I better do? I have an idea. Please, are you in?

AUNT.   Haven't you gone yet?

NEPHEW.   Oh, yes. I went as far as the end of the lane, but I forgot to tell you something, so I came back.

TARO.   That will be a very good plan, sir.

LORD.   Then I shall go.   You accompany me.

TARO.   Very well.

LORD.   Come!

TARO.   I am coming!

LORD.   When my wife in the province hears this good news, she will be waiting for my home-coming day and night.

TARO.   She must, indeed.
          Oh, sir, we are already here.   Shall I announce your arrival? Please wait here.

LORD.   All right.

TARO.   Please, your lord has come.

MISTRESS.   *Ha!*   There is an unfamiliar voice outside.
          Oh, is that you, Taro?   My lord is here, did you say?

TARO.   Yes, madam.

MISTRESS.   Oh!   This is most unexpected.   Pray, what lucky wind has brought you here?   How have you been?   As I had not seen you for a long while, I had certain misgivings.

LORD.   Oh, I am happy to find you well.   I have not seen you for a long while, have I?
          By the by, Taro boy, shall I tell her about our news?

TARO.   I believe there is no harm in telling her that.

MISTRESS.   What could it be?   Oh, I have fears.

LORD.   Oh, no!   It is nothing very important.   We have been in the capital for a long while about the lawsuit, but finally it was decided in our favor today.   As I must be going home soon, I came to say farewell.

MISTRESS.   Alas, what do I hear?   Going back home!   Then I shall not be able to see you again.   How sad this is!   (*She secretly draws to her a little water basin in the writing box.   Putting a few drops on her face, she pretends to cry bitterly.*)

LORD. Your deep grief touches me, but even if I go home, I shall be coming back soon. Therefore be of good cheer and wait for me. (*He weeps too.*)

MISTRESS. You say so now, but once back home, you will not even think of me. This is very sad indeed.

TARO. What do I see? I thought she was really crying, but she is just putting water on her face. What an odious shrew she is!

Pardon me, my lord! Will you come this way just a moment?

LORD. What is the matter?

TARO. Do you think she is really weeping? If you do, you are wrong. That's only plain water from the writing box.

LORD. Don't talk such nonsense to me! The poor thing is really crying because she must part with me.

MISTRESS. Oh, my dear lord! Where have you gone? 'Tis only a little while we can be together. Please come here.

LORD. I am sorry. Taro boy had something to tell me, so I went over there. The fool was talking nonsense.

TARO. It's incredible not to see through the woman's trick. Well, I have a scheme. We will see who is right. (*Removing the water basin, he puts an ink-well in its place.*)

MISTRESS. I am so loath to part with you even a few hours, but now this is going to be our last meeting! Oh, so very sad and miserable!

TARO. This is fun. Not knowing my trick, now she is putting ink all over her face. Just look at that face!

Oh, please, my lord! Will you step this way just a moment?

LORD. What is the matter?

TARO. Because you did not believe what I told you, I replaced the water basin with an ink-well. Just look at that face, please!

Eat you up, eat you up! Growl, growl! Eat you up! One more cup! Another! Delicious!

Boo, boo! I am a devil! Head first in a single bite. *Ha, ha!* What a fool a woman is! What is that I see over there on the wall? Nothing, nothing! I am getting exceedingly happy.

Eat you up! Fearful? Of course, I am a devil, and if a devil is not fearful, what is? One more drink? Another, another! Alas, no more is left in the cask? Just a few last drops! *yum, yum!*

E-a-t y-o-u u-p! D-e-v-o-u-r y-o-u!

AUNT.   How dreadful, how dreadful! I thought my nephew was teasing me, but this is a real and live devil. However it is getting very quiet in the house. Let me peek in! Maybe the devil is gone. Ah, what? Devil? Nothing! It is my own nephew and there he sleeps. This is most provoking. Because I refused to treat him, he swindled me.

What a hateful scoundrel you are! Get up, get up!

NEPHEW.   E-a-t y-o-u u-p! De-vour y-o-u!

AUNT.   What? you wretch! I am going to beat you into a pulp! Into a pulp!

NEPHEW.   Pardon! Ouch, ouch! Oh, oh! Please forgive me.

AUNT.   Beat you into a pulp, into a pulp! Oh, oh, is there no one around? Don't let him get away. Catch him, catch him!

THE BAG OF PARTING
(*Itoma-bukuro*)

Characters: THE MASTER, TARO, *his house-boy*, THE MASTER'S WIFE.

MASTER. I am the master of this house. My wife, whom I have known ever since we were so high, unfortunately, is not only exceedingly homely but also is a hopeless drag on me. For instance, she never gets up in the morning, and if she does once in a great while, she eats an enormous breakfast and berates me. But worst of all, she drinks and behaves outrageously. Indeed, she has been the bane of my existence, and I have been thinking of divorcing her for a long while.

Luckily, my wife went to visit her family yesterday and has not come home yet; this is a heaven-sent opportunity. I will send a notice of divorce by Taro and put an end to all my misery. I must first call Taro boy.

Yai, yai! Is Taro boy around?

TARO. *Ha!*

MASTER. Where are you?

TARO. In your presence.

MASTER. It is nothing very special that I called you for. As you know, my wife is an impossible shrew, and since I have exhausted my patience I wish to divorce her. Take this note to her.

TARO. I should very much like to oblige you, but as you know, her ladyship is different from other ladies. She is not going to accept your note so easily as that. You must excuse me from this errand.

MASTER. Oh, that's all right. Don't worry about it. I need no answer. Just leave the note and come back.

123

FIRST VISITOR.   I am a villager who dwells in this vicinity.   I
   am on my way to do an errand.   But the sky turns dark suddenly, and I fear it is going to rain.   I will stop at my temple
   and borrow an umbrella.   Oh, here I am.   Please!   Please!

NOVICE.   How do you do?   I am very happy to see you.

FIRST VISITOR.   I have been neglecting to call, but how is the
   priest?   And you?   I hope you are both well.

NOVICE.   We are both very well.   By the by, the priest has
   decided to retire, giving me full responsibility for the temple.
   Please come often.

FIRST VISITOR.   I congratulate you!   Had I known, I should
   have come especially to wish you success.

   As to my present visit, I was on my way to the village, but
   suddenly it looked as if it were going to rain.   Could you let
   me have an umbrella?

NOVICE.   Certainly.   Please wait a moment.

FIRST VISITOR.   Oh!   Very many thanks.

NOVICE.   Here, then!   I will let you have this.

FIRST VISITOR.   Thank you so much.

NOVICE.   If there is anything of any kind that I can do for you,
   please let me know.

FIRST VISITOR.   Certainly.   I will call on you for assistance.

NOVICE.   Are you going?

FIRST VISITOR.   Yes.   Good-bye!

NOVICE.   Good-bye!

FIRST VISITOR.   I am much obliged to you.

NOVICE.   I am glad you came in.

FIRST VISITOR.   Ah!   Well!   I am glad I did.
   Now I must hurry.

NOVICE.   The priest told me to let him know if any of the
   patrons came.   I will go and tell him.
   Please, sir!   Are you in?

PRIEST.   Yes, I am here.

NOVICE.   You must be feeling very dull.

PRIEST.   No, not very.

NOVICE.   Somebody has just been here.

PRIEST.   Did he come to worship, or was it that he had some business?

NOVICE.   He came to borrow an umbrella, and I let him have one.

PRIEST.   That was quite right, but tell me. Which umbrella did you let him have?

NOVICE.   The new one that we got the other day.

PRIEST.   You are a careless fellow. Would anybody ever dream of lending an umbrella which I have not used yet? The case will present itself again. When you do not wish to lend it, you can always find a good excuse.

NOVICE.   What would you say?

PRIEST.   You should say: "It would be no trouble to lend it to you, but recently my master went out with it and encountered a gust of wind at the crossing. The storm tore the ribs and the cover apart. So I tied them both by the middle and hung them up to the ceiling. I am afraid they would be of little use to you." You should say something like that, with an air of truth about it.

NOVICE.   I understand. Next time I shall certainly remember what you have told me.

    Now I must go.

PRIEST.   Must you go? Good-bye!

NOVICE.   Good-bye!

    That is very queer. Whatever my master says, it does seem strange to refuse to lend a thing when you have it by you.

SECOND VISITOR.   I live in this vicinity. As I have to go to a far-off place, I mean to stop at the temple and borrow a horse. I will go quickly. Ah! Here I am. Please! Please!

WIFE.   Don't flatter yourself thinking that I still have a little love for you.   I only came back to get one thing.

MASTER.   What is that?

WIFE.   A thing big enough to go into this bag.

MASTER.   Oh, I am willing to give you that much.   Get it. But first what is it?

WIFE.   That thing there!   (*She points toward the right.*)

MASTER.   Which one?   (*He turns around.*)

WIFE.   This is the thing I want.   (*So saying, she puts the bag on her husband's head and pulls the string.*)

MASTER.   Hey, hey!   What are you doing?   I can't see.   You are strangling me.   Murder! murder!   Forgive me, forgive me!

WIFE.   What?   Forgive you?   Nothing of the kind.   I am going to take you to a good place and give you what you deserve.

MASTER.   What misery!   Listen, I won't divorce you, so please forgive me.   Oh, please, please!

THE WOUNDED HIGHWAYMAN
(*Teoi Yamadachi*)

Characters: A HIGHWAYMAN, A PRIEST, THE HIGHWAYMAN'S WIFE.

HIGHWAYMAN.   I am a notorious highwayman who resides in this neighborhood.   From my childhood I disregarded my parents' wise counsel and idled away my youth.   Now I have no trade to support my family, so I practice robbery on this highway.   I am waiting here today.   Pray, let someone come this way, and I will strip him to his bare skin!   First I shall hide behind this bush.

PRIEST.   I am a priest who dwells in the Eastern District, and as I have not seen the imperial capital, I decided to take this trip.   First I shall do a little sightseeing and then makean extended pilgrimage in the western country.   I must hasten.

As it has often been said, unless one travels in his youth, he has nothing to remember in his old age.   The truth of the saying has prompted me to take this trip.   Well, where is this? Ah, Akasaka in the province of Mino, I see!   Already the sun is going down.   Though I should like to find a lodging, there is not a house in sight.   A little further and I may find one.   I must hasten.

HIGHWAYMAN.   *Ha!* there comes a priest.   I will strip him.

Hey, unholy priest!   You cannot pass through here.   Hand me over your money bag and strip at once.

PRIEST.   This certainly is very troublesome.   A poor pilgrim like me has nothing of any use to you.   I have been travelling on alms.   Please let me go.

THIRD VISITOR.   I have not called on you for a long time.   I hope both the priest and you have been well.

NOVICE.   Oh, yes! We both continue well.   By the by, I do not know what prompted the priest, but suddenly he has turned the whole responsibility of the temple to me and retired. I hope you will come as often as before.

THIRD VISITOR.   I congratulate you indeed.   Had I known it, I should have come especially to congratulate you.

Today I came on business.   Tomorrow is the religious anniversary of our family, and I shall be greatly honored if both the priest and you can come.

NOVICE.   To be sure, I can.   As to the priest, I am afraid he cannot come.

THIRD VISITOR.   Has he a previous engagement?

NOVICE.   No! But recently we have been putting him out to spring grass, and he has gone stark mad and has broken his hip bone.   At present he is lying in the corner of the stable under a straw mat.   I fear he is not going to be of very much service to you.

THIRD VISITOR.   But it is the priest that I am talking about.

NOVICE.   Precisely! I am speaking about the priest.

THIRD VISITOR.   Well! I am very sorry to hear that.   Then you will come?

NOVICE.   Most certainly, I will come.

THIRD VISITOR.   Now I must go.

NOVICE.   Must you?   Good-bye!

THIRD VISITOR.   Well, well! He says things that I cannot make out at all.

NOVICE.   This time I did as I was instructed, and the priest ought to be pleased.

If you please, are you in?

PRIEST.   Yes, I am in.   Is it on business that you come?

NOVICE. Somebody has just been here to ask both you and me to go to him tomorrow to attend a religious anniversary in his family. So I said that I would go, but that you would hardly be able to do so.

PRIEST. Luckily I have no engagement tomorrow, and I should like to go.

NOVICE. But I said what you had instructed me to say.

PRIEST. I do not remember. What did you tell him?

NOVICE. I said that you had been put out to spring grass, but had gone stark mad and broken your hip bone. At present you were lying in the corner of the stable under a straw mat. I said I feared that you could not come.

PRIEST. Did you really and truly say that to him?

NOVICE. Yes! Really and truly.

PRIEST. Well, I never! Say what you will, you are a perfect dunce. No matter how many times I say a thing, nothing seems to make you understand. I told you to say that when anyone came to borrow a horse.

The end of all this is that it will never do for you to become a priest. Get out!

NOVICE. Oh!

PRIEST. Won't you get out? Won't you get out? Won't you?

NOVICE. Ouch! ouch! o-u-c-h!

But, sir! Even if you are my master, it is a great shame for you to beat me like this. For all you are the man you are, you cannot tell me that you have not gone stark mad.

PRIEST. When have I ever gone stark mad? If I ever was, out with it quick! Out with it!

NOVICE. If I were to tell it, you would be put to shame.

PRIEST. I know of nothing that could put me to shame. If there is, out with it quick, quick!

NOVICE. Well then, I will tell it.

Oh, sir priest, my husband came home with a gaping wound. Will you say a few prayers for him?

PRIEST. I am most sorry to hear it, my good lady. Indeed I will pray for your husband. It is a part of my duty.

Oh, thou merciful Amidha Buddha, Amidha Buddha . . . !

HIGHWAYMAN. Quick! This is the priest who murdered me. Hand me the sword! Do not let him get away.

WIFE. What! You scoundrel! Catch him!

PRIEST. How unfortunate! To pick out this particular house to stay in! Such is my luck! Dreadful, dreadful!

HIGHWAYMAN. Come, wife, run after him quickly! Beat him to death. Don't let him get away!

PRIEST. Help, help!

HIGHWAYMAN AND WIFE. Catch him! Don't let him get away!

THE FAMILY QUARREL
(*Mizu-ron Muko*)

Characters: A FATHER-IN-LAW, A SON-IN-LAW, HIS WIFE.

FATHER-IN-LAW.   I am a peasant who dwells in the village. The rice crop this year is doing uncommonly well, and I am very happy.   But we have been having very dry weather, and the rice paddies are getting too dry.   That is the reason why I have been visiting my fields every day.

Well, why doesn't it rain?   What stubborn weather!   Oh! As I have strolled along, I am already here.   My crop is beautiful.   What?   I fixed the lock-house so that the water would flow into my fields, but it is turned off on my side and is going into the next paddies.   This is indeed provoking. But the next fields belong to none other than my son-in-law· The sly old dog!   That he, of all men, should do such a thing! Well, I have fixed it.   Now it is flowing into mine fast.   In a season like this, even in the family, one must be on his guard. I will keep watch here.

SON-IN-LAW.   I am a peasant who dwells in this vicinity. Really this is a most prosperous year, and the crop is excellent. The recent dry weather is, however, a bit disconcerting.   The fields are drying up fast, and I must keep close watch and not neglect them.   I do hope it is going to rain soon, and then all will be well with the world.   But the weather is contrary.

Here I am in my own fields.   Marvelous sight!   Unlike some others, mine are superb.   What is this?   My side of the lock-house is closed up, and all the water is flowing in the other side, which belongs to none other than my father-in-law.   How unreasonable!

FATHER.   Oh, hello! You have come, too.

SON.   Yes, I thought I'd come and have a look.

FATHER.   It doesn't rain, does it?

SON.   Indeed it doesn't.

FATHER.   I hear there was a meeting in the village hall last night. What was it about?

SON.   Weren't you there? It was nothing special, but as the drought is getting serious, the mayor got us together to see what we had better do. There were all sorts of suggestions made. Some said we should propitiate the gods by dancing before the shrine, and some said we might offer a wrestling match. No one could agree and for a while the meeting became very lively. But finally the mayor suggested that a dance would perhaps be the best, and we decided upon that.

FATHER.   The mayor certainly has a good memory. A long time ago when there was a bad drought, we had a gorgeous dance, and it rained right away. It was very effective.

SON.   Now I remember it. Well, the young fellows began to practice the dance steps then, and we also ordered the costumes. It was quite exciting.

FATHER.   *Yai, yai!* What are you doing?

SON.   Oh, nothing! I was just drawing a little water into my fields, too.

FATHER.   I thought someone played me a dirty trick a while ago. It was you, was it? They say a father-in-law is just like one's father, but certainly that is not the way you treat your own father, I hope.

SON.   Now, look here. I am your son-in-law, and they say a son-in-law is as good as one's own son. Then it is not fair to take all the water from your son's paddy fields, is it? Really, even if your paddy fields dry up like stone, you should give water to your son.

FATHER.   You rascal! You cannot monopolize all the water.

SON.   In a season like this, he who gets it has it.   That's my motto.

FATHER.   All right! if that is the way you feel about it.   I will get it and have it, too.

Hey, why do you squirt water on my face?

SON.   Sorry!   That was pure accident.

FATHER.   If that was an accident, this is, too.

SON.   It was, but you are doing it purposely.   Here's another accident.

FATHER.   Another accident?   Hey, you threw sand at me. You can't treat me like that.

SON.   Oh, you threw mud at me.

FATHER.   After all this, I shan't let you off so easily.

SON.   Nor I you.   My patience is exhausted.

WIFE.   Oh, oh, how sad!   My father and husband are fighting. What had I better do?   Is no one around?   Please stop them.

SON.   Hey, my wife!   Come and pull your father's leg.

WIFE.   Very well.   I obey.

SON.   I have won, you dear, dear girl!   Come here.   Come to me.

WIFE.   Hello, Papa!   We'll come and call on you at the next festival.

FATHER.   You will, will you?   You rascals, treating your father like this.   Is there no one around?   Catch them!   Do not let them get away!

THUNDER GOD
(*Kaminari*)

Characters: A MOUNTEBANK, THUNDER GOD, CHORUS.

MOUNTEBANK.　　A mock medicine man without medicine
　　　　　　　　Whose only trust is Kiwada[1] pills!

I am a mountebank who dwells in Kyoto.　Though I have had various and sundry patients, I have always been financially embarrassed.　Now I go to a far-off country to try my fortune, and that is the reason I am here.　I shall walk leisurely.

Indeed in this imperial reign when peace and prosperity rule, there are too many wonderful doctors, such as court physicians, official medicine men, and others; and a quack like me has no chance.　There is nothing for me to do but move away.

Ah!　As I amble along, I am already in a wide open field, but I do not know where it is.　Well, well!　Where can this be?　Oh, I know.　This is Innami Plain of Harima Province, of which I have often heard.　But look!　How unfortunate! The sky is suddenly overcast and looks very terrifying.　Now rain is coming down, and it is most troublesome, indeed. Moreover, thunder is roaring.　What had I better do to find a shelter?

THUNDER GOD.　　*Bang, bang!　Clap, clap!*

MOUNTEBANK.　　Oh, mercy!　Heaven protect me from thunder and lightning!

THUNDER.　　Oh, how painful, painful!　Ouch, ouch!
　　Well, well!　I have bruised my hip bones very badly and am

[1] Phellodendron amurensis *Rupr.*, the bark of which was used as herb.

134

unable to get up to Heaven. There is not even a tree in sight to support me. *Ha!* There is someone stooping down. What are you there?

MOUNTEBANK.   I am a human being.

THUNDER.   Even if you are a human being, what kind are you?

MOUNTEBANK.   I am a quack. On my way to a distant country I was passing through this plain, and as it thundered so terrifically, I was frightened out of my wits, and I am crouching here in this corner.

THUNDER.   What? You are a quack?

MOUNTEBANK.   Indeed I am.

THUNDER.   I am the Thunder God, but by some mishap I tripped and fell here. I fear I have bruised my hip bones badly and cannot even turn around. I hope you will treat me.

MOUNTEBANK.   Well, although I am honored, I have been treating human beings all this while, and never had any experience with the Thunder God. Hence as regards that matter, you must excuse me.

THUNDER.   Well, should you refuse, I will pinch you to death.

MOUNTEBANK.   Oh, if that is the case, I will treat you. Please spare my life.

THUNDER.   Now then, treat me at once.

MOUNTEBANK.   First of all I shall feel your pulse.

THUNDER.   Please feel my pulse. But what under the sun are you doing?

MOUNTEBANK.   That's all right. Be at ease. With the creatures that inhabit this lowly earth, their hands are the key to their heart, liver, kidney, lungs, spleen — in short, to all their life organs; but you, the noble heavenly being, have your key in your head. Therefore I am going to feel your pulse on the top of your head.

THUNDER.   I see, of course.

MOUNTEBANK.   Your falling from Heaven like this was not pure accident. You are suffering from a very acute attack of palsy, and that was the cause.

THUNDER.   You are very clever in your diagnosis. Very good indeed! I have been suffering from a chronic attack of palsy.

MOUNTEBANK.   That I clearly see.

THUNDER.   Then please treat me right away.

MOUNTEBANK.   Very well. Unfortunately we are in the midst of a wild plain. There is no way of my making the herb medicine. As I also practice the acupuncture, under the circumstances that will be the best and quickest method. I will treat you with the needle.

THUNDER.   That's reasonable. Treat me well so that I can return to heaven speedily.

MOUNTEBANK.   Very well. Here it goes! *Bang, bang! Push, push!*

THUNDER.   Painful, painful! Ouch, ouch! Help, help!

MOUNTEBANK.   A Thunder God like you should not be such a coward. Bear it patiently, sir.
    Bang, bang! Push, push! How was this one?

THUNDER.   That was not so bad.

MOUNTEBANK.   This time I am going to give you a side-needle.

THUNDER.   Good! But please do it so that it will not hurt very much.

MOUNTEBANK.   It is only a short while. Be a good sport!
    Bang, bang! Push, push!

THUNDER.   Help, help! This is terrible. Ouch, ouch! Painful, painful!

MOUNTEBANK.   Now, now, if you twist your body so, the needles will all go in crooked. Turn this way a little. How is it? Do you feel any better?

THUNDER.   Ah! I am feeling a little better.

MOUNTEBANK.   This time I am going to try needles in your hip.

THUNDER.   Do it gently, please.

MOUNTEBANK.   Oh, don't be such a coward. *Bang, bang! Push, push!*

THUNDER.   Ouch, ouch! Painful, painful! Oh, oh!

MOUNTEBANK.   *Bang, bang! Bang, bang!*
How is it now?

THUNDER.   I am all well now.

MOUNTEBANK.   Congratulations! I am very happy to hear of your speedy recovery.

THUNDER.   You are exceedingly skillful in the art of medicine. Among my colleagues, there are several who suffer from palsy. I wish you could treat them, too.

MOUNTEBANK.   If I treat them only once, they will be cured of that malady for the rest of their lives.

THUNDER.   I have no doubt. Now I would like to reward you liberally, but unfortunately I have nothing with me. What had I better do?

MOUNTEBANK.   You are very kind. The fact you are restored to health is in itself a sufficient reward for a physician. I need no other.

THUNDER.   Nevertheless I should like to give you something! How about this drumstick?

MOUNTEBANK.   Thank you very much, but I have no use for it.

THUNDER.   Then what can I give you? How about this drum?

MOUNTEBANK.   No, thank you. That would get me in trouble on the earth.

THUNDER.   But I want to give you something. What had I better do? If you have any wish, do tell me. I will grant it.

MOUNTEBANK.   I am greatly obliged to you. As you see my profession forces me to walk about in the country much, and I shall be very grateful if you could let the sun shine when it ought to and let the rain fall when it should. Then there will be neither drought nor flood; all the grains will be ripe in season, and we shall be prosperous.

THUNDER. That is very easy. But for how long shall I keep this promise?

MOUNTEBANK. Please keep it for three thousand years.

THUNDER. No, no, three thousand years are too long. I will observe it for three years.

MOUNTEBANK. In the world below three years are nothing. That is too short. Please keep it for one thousand years.

THUNDER. Oh, no! One thousand is still too long. How about eight hundred years?

MOUNTEBANK. I am greatly obliged to you. Then please keep this promise for eight hundred years.

THUNDER. I will make an end to all droughts and floods so that harvests will be abundant; also I will grant you much happiness and long life.

MOUNTEBANK. My gratitude exceeds my words.

THUNDER. I am ascending to Heaven now.

MOUNTEBANK. I am sorry we have to part.

CHORUS. Rain and sunshine,
Sunshine and rain!
No more flood and no more drought
For eight hundred long years!
Thou Mountebank, incarnate of Yakushi-nyorai,
August god of medicine, who cured my palsy
Farewell! Fare thee well!

So saying the Thunder God ascended to heavenward.

THUNDER. *Bang, bang! Clap, clap!*

MOUNTEBANK. Oh, mercy! Heaven protect me from thunder and lightning!

BIBLIOGRAPHY
Western

Aston, William George, 1841–1911.

A HISTORY OF JAPANESE LITERATURE. New York, D. Appleton, 1899. xi, 408 pp. (*Half-title:* Short histories of the literatures of the world, ed. by E. Gosse.) "Bibliographical note": pp. 400–402. "A list of dictionaries, grammars, and other works of reference useful to students of Japanese": p. 403.

Bénazet, Alexandre, 1890–

LE THÉÂTRE AU JAPON: esquisse d'une histoire littéraire . . . Paris, E. Leroux, 1901. xiii, 11–296 pp. illus., plates. "Bibliographie du théâtre": pp. 289–294.

Florenz, Karl Adolf, 1865–

GESCHICHTE DER JAPANISCHEN LITTERATUR. Leipzig, C. F. Amelang, 1909. 3 p. 1., iii–x, 642 pp. (*Added title page:* Die Litteraturen des Ostens in Einzeldarstellungen. 10. bd.)

Gersdorff, Wolfgang, *freiherr von*, 1876–

JAPANISCHE DRAMEN, FÜR DIE DEUTSCHE BÜHNE. Jena, Diedericks, 1926. 205 pp., incl. plates.

Lombard, Frank Alanson, 1872–

AN OUTLINE HISTORY OF THE JAPANESE DRAMA, with an introduction by George Pierce Baker. London, G. Allen & Unwin, 1928. 358, 1 p., incl. illus., plates. "Authorities": pp. 353–354.

Noguchi, Yone, tr.

TEN KIOGEN IN ENGLISH. Tokyo, The Tozaisha, 1907. 193 pp.

Sadler, Arthur Lindsay, 1882–

JAPANESE PLAYS: NO–KYÔGEN–KABUKI. Sydney, Angus & Robertson, 1934. xxvi, 283 pp. illus., incl. plans.

Shimoi, Harukichi.

KYÔGEN, antiche farse giapponesi con numerose illustrazioni antiche e una introduzione di H. Shimoi. Neapel, Collana dei Rami Fioriti di SAKURA. no. 3, 1920.

Japanese

I. *Texts:*

KYÔGEN–KI [Collection of *kyôgen*]. Edo, 1848. 15 books with 150 plays. illus.

> This is a reprint of the 1699–1700 edition. Hence texts are those of the *Izumi* school.

KYÔGEN NIJU–BAN [Twenty *kyôgen*], ed. by Yaichi Haga. *Shuchin meicho bunko*. Tokyo, Fuzanbo, 1903. 2d ed.

> The basis of Dr. Haga's texts is a manuscript of the *Sagi* school.

KYÔGEN ZENSHU [A complete collection of *kyôgen*], ed. by Nariyuki Koda. Tokyo, Hakubunkan, 1903. 3 v. illus.

> Dr. Koda took the printed texts of 1699–1700 and 1730 of the *Izumi* school as the basis for this work, but he also had access to excellent manuscript texts of the *Ôkura* school, in the possession of Zennosuke Yasuda. Therefore, when there was a difference in story or diction between two schools, he was able to give the texts of both. For this reason, this is the most satisfactory edition we now have for students of *kyôgen*.

KYÔGEN-KI [Collection of *kyôgen*], ed. by Hachiro Nomura. *Yûhôdo bunko.* Tokyo, 1917. 2 v., with 200 plays. illus., plates.

Texts are of the *Izumi* school. Besides the original 150 plays, the editor added 50 more which were collected from the 18th century sources.

KYÔGEN SHUSEI [Cyclopaedia of *kyôgen*], ed. by Kaizô Nonomura and Tsunejirô Andô. Tokyo, Shunyodo, 1931. illus., plates.

Of 734 interludes included in the present edition, strictly speaking there are only about 250 *kyôgen.* The rest are either slightly different versions of the old *kyôgen* or the later parodies of the *Nô* plays. The texts in general are of the *Izumi* school, with a few from the *Sagi* and the *Ôkura* schools.

II. *Articles:*

BUNAN DENGAKU NO NÔ KI [A description of the *dengaku Nô* performance in the Bunan era (1444–1448)], by Priest Jitsu. *Gunsho ruijû.* v. 19, pp. 712–717.

KYÔGEN NO KENKYÛ [Study of *kyôgen*], by Katashi Sasano. *Nihon bungaku kôza.* Tokyo, 1932. v. 7, pp. 347–377.

KYÔGEN NO KEITAI RON [Form and structure of *kyôgen*], by Katashi Sasano. *Kokugo to kokubun-gaku.* v. 8, no. 10, pp. 1650–1678.

NIHON GEKIJÔ ZU-SHI [Illustrated history of the Japanese theatre], by Yoshitaro Takeuchi. v. 1. Tokyo, Mibushoin, 1935.

SARUGAKU ENKAKU KÔ [Evolution of *sarugaku*], by Shigeyasu Kawasaki (1799–1832). *Onchi sôsho.* Tokyo, 1891. v. 8, pp. 1–30.

SARUGAKU DENKI [History of *sarugaku*], *Onchi sôsho.* v. 12, pp. 1–72.

SEAMI JÛROKU–BU SHÛ, by Motokiyo Seami (1363–1444); edited by Kaizô Nonomura. Tokyo, 1926.

TADASU GAWARA KWANJIN SARUGAKU NIKKI [Diary of the benefit *sarugaku* performance in the Tadasu Gawara], by Sogo Ise. *Gunsho ruijû.* v. 19, pp. 717–721.

See also IHON TADASU GAWARA KWANJIN SARU-GAKU NIKKI, a memorandum by one Shigechika Ushio, addressed to Zenbei Shishido, who was a tea master. *Gunsho ruijû.* v. 19, pp. 722–723.

A LIST OF TRANSLATIONS OF KYÔGEN

1. AKUBÔ. The Priest and the Knave, trans. by Masujiro Honda and Frank Backus Williams. *Oriental Review* April 1913, v. 3, no. 6, pp. 427–429.

2. AKUTARÔ. Trans. by A. L. Sadler. *Japanese Plays*, pp. 150–151.

3. ASAHINA. Trans. by A. L. Sadler. *Japanese Plays*, pp. 92–95.

4. BÔSHIBARI. Pinioned. *The Chrysanthemum*, Aug. 1882, v. 2, no. 8, pp. 353–361.

5. BUSSHI. The Buddha-maker, trans. by A. L. Sadler. *Japanese Plays*, pp. 146–149.

6. BUSU. Somebody-nothing: an ancient Japanese farce, trans. by Michio Itow and Louis V. Ledoux. *Asia*, Dec. 1921, v. 21, no. 12, pp. 1011–1012.
   _____. (*A kyôgen*) trans. by Frank Alanson Lombard. *Outline History of Japanese Drama*, pp. 164–171.
   _____. Le Poison, trans. by Noël Péri. "Farces japonaises." *Japon et Extrême Orient*, April 1924, v. 1, no. 5, pp. 385–393.
   _____. (A farce) "Around the Hibachi." *Japan Magazine*, June 1915, v. 6, no. 2, pp. 115–117. Summary.

7. CHA-TSUBO. Vaso di thè, un kyôgen-farsa antica, trans. by Harukichi Shimoi and Rodolfo Vingiani. *Sakura*, v. 1, 1920, pp. 71–73.

8. DOBU–KACCHIRI. The Two Blind Men, trans. by Yone Noguchi. *Ten Kiogen in English*, pp. 48–67. Text in Japanese.

143

DOBU–KACCHIRI. The Two Blind Men, trans. by Yone Noguchi. *The Yōkyokukai.* Jan. 1917, v. 6, no. 1, pp. 4–8.

9. DŌJŌJI (Mibu version). Summary translation by Frank Alanson Lombard. *Outline History of Japanese Drama*, pp. 176–178.

10. DONTARŌ. Trans. by A. L. Sadler. *Japanese Plays*, pp. 133–135.

_____. Summary translation by Oswald G. Tuck. "Some Comic Medieval Plays of Japan." *Transactions and Proceedings of the Japan Society*, London. 1924, v. 21, p. 4.

11. EBISU DAIKOKU. Ebisu and Daikoku, trans. by A. L. Sadler. *Japanese Plays*, pp. 71–72.

12. ESASHI JŌWŌ. The Fowler, trans. by A. L. Sadler. *The Far East*, Oct. 8, 1921, v. 23, no. 492, pp. 359–360.

_____. _____, _____. *Japanese Plays*, pp. 109–111.

_____. The Bird-catcher in Hell, trans. by Arthur Waley. *Nō Plays of Japan*, pp. 255–259.

_____. _____, _____. "The Columbia University Course in Literature." *The Wisdom of the East.* Founders edition. New York, Columbia University Press, 1928. v. 1, pp. 559–561. Reprinted from the *Nō Plays of Japan.*

13. FUSE NAI. Pas d'aumône, trans. by Noël Péri. "Farces japonaises." *Japan et Extrême Orient*, Sept. 1924, v. 2, no. 9, pp. 148–156.

14. HAGI DAIMYŌ. Trans. by Karl A. Florenz. *Geschichte der japanischen Litteratur*, pp. 411–415.

15. HANAKO. (ZAZEN) Abstraction, trans. by Basil Hall Chamberlain. *Literature of the Orient.* London, Colonial Press, 1902. v. 8, pp. 283–296.

_____. A Man and His Wife, trans. by Colin Campbell Clements. "Seven Plays of Old Japan." *Poet-Lore*, Summer 1920, v. 31, no. 2, pp. 197–203.

HANAKO. (ZAZEN) Die Busse, trans. by Wolfgang von Gersdorff. *Japanische Dramen*, pp. 152–178.

———. Mademoiselle Hana, trans. by Noël Péri. "Farces japonaises." *Japon et Extrême Orient*, May–June 1924, v. 1, no. 6, pp. 494–500.

———. Fraulein Hana, Japanische Farce, trans. by Noël Péri. *Der Querschnitt*. Nov. 1924, v. 4, no. 5, pp. 288–293. Reprinted from *Japon et Extrême Orient*.

———. Trans. by A. L. Sadler. *Japanese Plays*, pp. 81–85.

16. HI NO SAKE. The Liquor-pipe, trans. by A. L. Sadler. *Japanese Plays*, pp. 136–140.

17. HONE–KAWA. Ribs and Skin, trans. by Basil Hall Chamberlain. "On the Medieval Colloquial Dialect of the Comedies." *Transactions of the Asiatic Society of Japan*, 1879, v. 6, part iii, pp. 383–396. Text in roman letters.

———. ———, ———. *Things Japanese*. London, John Murray, 1902. pp. 196–204.

———. (KOPPI) Les os et la peau, tr. by Noël Péri. "Farces japonaises." *Japon et Extrême Orient*, May–June 1934, v. 1, no. 6, pp. 485–493.

———. The Ribs and the Cover, trans. by Shio Sakanishi. The *Golden Book Magazine*, March 1932, v. 15, no. 87, pp. 263–265.

18. HÔRAKU WARI. The Breaking of the Plates. Summary translation by Frank Alanson Lombard. *Outline History of Japanese Drama*, pp. 175–176.

19. ISHIGAMI. The Stone God, trans. by A. L. Sadler. *Japanese Plays*, pp. 78–80.

20. ITOMA–BUKURO. The Bag of Leave-taking, trans. by A. L. Sadler. *Japanese Plays*, pp. 67–70.

21. KAKI URI. The Persimmon-seller, trans. by A. L. Sadler. *Japanese Plays*, pp. 96–99.

22. KAKI YAMABUSHI. The Persimmon Friar. Summary translation by Oswald G. Tuck. "Some Comic Medieval Plays of Japan." *Transactions and Proceedings of the Japan Society*, London, 1924, v. 21, p. 8.

23. KAMA–PPARA. Un Coup de Serpe dans le Ventre, trans. by Noël Péri. "Farces japonaises." *Japon et Extrême Orient*. April 1924, v. 1, no. 5, pp. 398–404.

24. KAMINARI. Thunder-God, trans. by Oswald G. Tuck. "Some Comic Medieval Plays of Japan." *Transactions and Proceedings of the Japan Society*, London. 1924, v. 21, pp. 6–7.

    ————. ————. The *Tourist*, Sept. 1932, v. 2, no. 9, pp. 51–56.

    ————. ————. "No" Drama. Nara, Nara Hotel, July 1930, pp. 1–4.

    ————. Dieu du Tonnerre. "Kyoghen" ou Drame. Nara, Nara Hotel, September 1930, p. 5.

25. KASA NO SHITA. Under the Hat, trans. by A. L. Sadler. *Japanese Plays*, pp. 115–119.

    ————. Under the Hat, a Nô Kyôgen. *The Far East*. Nov. 12, 1921, no. 497, pp. 79, 82.

26. KITSUNE TZUKI. Kitzne Tsouki, La possession par les renards. Summary by Alexandre Bénazet. *Le Théâtre au Japon*, pp. 123–124.

27. KITSUNE–ZUKA. The Fox Hill, trans. by Yone Yoguchi. *Ten Kiogen in English*, pp. 98–119. Text in Japanese.

    ————. The Fox's Grave, trans. by Michio Itow and Louis V. Ledoux. *The Outlook*, Feb. 14, 1923, v. 133, pp. 306–308.

28. KO NUSUBITO. The Thief and the Child, trans. by A. L. Sadler. *Japanese Plays*, pp. 106–108.
    KOPPI, *see* HONE–KAWA.

29. KOSHI–INORI. Loin Prayer of Yamabushi. "No" Drama. Nara, Nara Hotel, July 1930, pp. 5–8.

30. KÔYAKU-NERI. The Ointment Vender, trans. by A. L. Sadler. *Japanese Plays*, pp. 120–123.

31. MIYAGE NO KAGAMI. The Gift Mirror, trans. by Yone Noguchi. *Ten Kiogen in English*, pp. 140–153. Text in Japanese.

32. MIZUKUMI SHINBOCHI. The Acolyte's Water-drawing, trans. by A. L. Sadler. *Japanese Plays*, pp. 127–129.

33. NAGÁMITSU. Trans. by Carlo Valenziani. *Filologia, Atti della Reale Accademia dei Lincei Rendiconti.* Roma, 1891. Series 4, v. 7, no. 1, pp. 301–308.

34. NININ DAIMYÔ, a Nô Kyôgen. Trans. by Eishirô Hori. *The Far East*, Dec. 25, 1920, v. 20, no. 452, pp. 334–336.

35. NIWÔ. Trans. by Yone Noguchi. *Ten Kiogen in English*, pp. 154–175. Text in Japanese.
_____. Le Ni-o, trans. by Noël Péri. "Farces japonaises." *Japon et Extrême Orient*, July-Aug. 1924, v. 2, no. 7–8, pp. 56–63.

36. NUKEGARA. The Demon's Shell, trans. by Yone Noguchi. *Poet-Lore*, Autumn 1906, v. 17, no. 3, pp. 44–49.
_____. _____, _____. *Ten Kiogen in English*, pp. 14–35. Text in Japanese.

37. OBA GA SAKÉ. Le Saké (eau-de-vie-de riz) de la Tante, trans. by Alexandre Bénazet. *Le Théâtre au Japon*, pp. 138–140.
_____. Aunty's Sake, trans. by Yone Noguchi. *Ten Kiogen in English*, pp. 14–35. Text in Japanese.

38. ONI-GAWARA. The Demon Tile, trans. by Yone Noguchi. *Ten Kiogen in English*, pp. 176–185. Text in Japanese.
_____. The Gargoyle, trans. by A. L. Sadler. *Japanese Plays*, pp. 141–142.

39. ONI NO TSUCHI. The Demon's Mallet, trans. by Yone Noguchi. *Ten Kiogen in English*, pp. 68–97. Text in Japanese.

40. RAKUAMI. Trans. by A. L. Sadler. *Japanese Plays*, pp. 124–126.

41. ROKUNIN SÔ. The Six Priests. *The Chrysanthemum*, May 1882, v. 2, no. 5, pp. 201–207.

———. Drei Tonsuren, ein Lustspiel, trans. by F. A. Junker von Langegg. "Alte japanische Dramen: I." *Das Magazin für die literatur des in- und Auslandes*, April 12, 19, 1884, v. 53, nos. 15–16, pp. 229–232, 250–251.

———. The Six Who Became Priests. *The New East*, Dec. 1918, v. 3, no. 6, pp. 577–578.

———. Tous religieux, trans. by Noël Péri. "Farces japonaises." *Japon et Extrême Orient*, Sept. 1924, v. 2, no. 9, pp. 156–163.

———. The Six Shavelings, trans. by A. L. Sadler. *Japanese Plays*, pp. 86–91.

42. ROKU JIZÔ. The Six Jizô. Summary by Osman Edwards. *Japanese Plays and Playfellows*, pp. 53–54.

———. ———. Summary by Alexandre Bénazet. *Le Théâtre au Japon*, pp. 129–130.

43. SAI NO KAWARA. The River of Fate. Summary translation by Frank Alanson Lombard. *Outline History of Japanese Drama*, pp. 178–179.

44. SANNIN KATAWA. The Three Cripples, trans. by Frank Brinkley. *Japan, Its History, Arts and Literature*. Boston & Tokyo, J. B. Millet, 1901. v. 3, pp. 52–59.

———. ———, trans. by Eishirô Hori. *The Far East*, April 2, 1921, v. 21, no. 465, pp. 350–352.

———. Les Trois Estropiats, trans. by Michel Revon. *Anthologie de la Littérature japonaise*. Paris, Delagrave, 1910. pp. 312–317.

———. The Three Deformed Men, trans. by Umeko Tsuda. *Eigo Seinen* (The Rising Generation), April 1, 15, 1913, v. 29, nos. 1–4, pp. 11, 43, 75, 107–108.

45. SHIBIRI. Pins and Needles, trans. by A. L. Sadler. *Japanese Plays*, pp. 100–101.

46. SHIKA–GARI. The Stag Hunter, trans. by A. L. Sadler. *Japanese Plays*, pp. 102–105.

47. SHU JYÔ. The Priest's Staff, a Nô Kyôgen, trans. by A. L. Sadler. *The Far East*, Sept. 17, 1921, v. 23, no. 489, p. 259.
——. The Priest's Staff, trans. by A. L. Sadler. *Japanese Plays*, pp. 112–114.

48. SÔHACHI. Trans. by Eishirô Hori. *The Far East*, Nov. 13, 1920, v. 20, no. 446, pp. 135–137.
——. Trans. by Noël Péri. "Farces japonaises." *Japon et Extrême Orient*, March 1924, v. 1, no. 4, pp. 310–321.

49. SUMI–NURI ONNA. The Ink Smear, trans. by Eishirô Hori. *The Far East*, Jan. 22, 1921, v. 20, no. 455, pp. 463–464.
——. Tinten blecken, ein Lustspiel, trans. by F. A. Junker von Langegg. "Alte japanische Dramen: II." *Das magazin für die literatur des in- und Auslandes*, June 14, 1884, v. 53, no. 24, pp. 374–380.
——. The Ink Woman, trans. by Yone Noguchi. *Ten Kiogen in English*, pp. 36–47. Text in Japanese.
——. La femme barvouillée d'encre, trans. by Noël Péri. "Farces japonaises." *Japon et Extrême Orient*, April 1924, v. 1, no. 5, pp. 394–397.
——. Ink-stained. *The Chrysanthemum*, July 1882, v. 2, no. 7, pp. 297–304.

50. SUÔ OTOSHI. The Lost Dress-coat. *Japan Magazine*, Nov. 1920, v. 11, no. 6, pp. 343–345.

51. SURIGAI KÔTÔ. The second-class master blindman and the monkey, trans. by A. L. Sadler. *Japanese Plays*, pp. 73–77.

52. TAKO. The Cuttle-fish, trans. by A. L. Sadler. *Japanese Plays*, pp. 130–132.

53. TSÛEN. Trans. by A. L. Sadler. *Japanese Plays*, pp. 143–145.

54. TSURI–KITSUNE. Le renard pris au piège, trans. by Noël Péri. "Farces japonaises." *Japon et Extrême Orient*. July–Aug. 1924, v. 2, no. 7–8, pp. 63–68.

55. TSURI ONNA. She Who Was Fished, trans. by Michio Itow and Louis V. Ledoux. *The Outlook*, Jan. 31, 1923, v. 133, pp. 218–219.

56. URI NUSUBITO. The Melon Thief, trans. by Yone Noguchi. *Poet-Lore*, Spring 1904, v. 15, no. 1, pp. 40–42.
    ____. ____, ____. *Ten Kiogen in English*, pp. 2–13. Text in Japanese.
    ____. ____, ____. *The Yôkyokukai*, Sept. 1916, v. 5, no. 3, pp. 7–9.
    ____. ____, trans. by Umeko Tsuda. *Eigo Seinen* (The Rising Generation), Feb. 15, March 1, 1913, v. 28, no. 10, 11, pp. 299, 329–330.
    ____. The Melon Thief, from a medieval Japanese farce, trans. by Shigeyoshi Obata. *Drama*, Dec. 1919, v. 10, no. 3, pp. 104–107.
    ____. The Melon Thief: from a medieval Japanese farce, trans. by Shigeyoshi Obata. New York, Samuel French, 1923. 20 p.

57. UTSUBO–ZARU. An interlude comedy, trans. by M. E. Hall. Kyoto. 7 pp. mimeographed.
    ____. The Quiver Monkey, trans. by Eishirô Hori. *The Far East*, Feb. 19, 1921, v. 21, no. 459, pp. 128–130.

58. YAO JIZÔ. Le Jizô de Yao, trans. by Noël Péri. "Farces japonaises." *Japon et Extrême Orient*, March 1924, v. 1, no. 4, pp. 322–326.

    ZAZEN, *see* HANAKO.